JANE PACKER
COLOUR

JANE PACKER
COLOUR

conran OCTOPUS

"No matter what the season, you'll find a colour to match your mood. Look closely at how I've chosen colours and textures that work together, ignite one another and look good in an almost inexplicable way. Play, abandon rules, embrace spontaneity – there's a new generation of flowers and colours out there."

Contents

8   LIST OF PROJECTS

10   INTRODUCTION

14   ## Red
SPRING *16* | SUMMER *24* | AUTUMN *32* | WINTER *38*

46   ## White
SPRING *48* | SUMMER *58* | AUTUMN *64* | WINTER *68*

74   ## Green
SPRING *76* | SUMMER *82* | AUTUMN *88* | WINTER *94*

100   ## Yellow
SPRING *102* | SUMMER *110* | AUTUMN *118* | WINTER *122*

126   ## Pink
SPRING *128* | SUMMER *136* | AUTUMN *144* | WINTER *148*

152   ## Blue
SPRING *154* | SUMMER *160* | AUTUMN *168* | WINTER *172*

176   FLOWER DIRECTORY

190   INDEX

192   ACKNOWLEDGEMENTS

List of projects

22   **No-bake cake**
A THREE-TIERED WEDDING 'CAKE' MADE FROM ROSES

30   **Pedestal arrangement**
A CORNUCOPIA OF COLOUR

44   **Berry wreath**
A FESTIVE DECORATION FOR INSIDE OR OUTSIDE

56   **All wrapped up**
THREE CLASSIC TALL AND ELEGANT DISPLAYS

63   **Dressed in flowers**
A SKIRT OF MIXED SUMMER FLOWERS

66   **Autumn wreath**
A CIRCLE OF OAK LEAVES AND PERRY PEARS FOR AUTUMN

86   **Green globe**
GREEN HYDRANGEAS AND TRAILING AMARNTHUS

92   **Topiary tree**
A 'TREE' MADE WITH BAMBOO AND SUNFLOWER HEADS

108   **Tulip bowl**
A CASCADE OF TULIPS

132   **Pink and silver urn**
A TROPHY OF SPRING PINKS

142   **Peony and rose garland**
A FLOWER GARLAND TO WEAR OR FOR THE HOME

166   **Have a heart**
A FLORAL SYMBOL OF LOVE

170   **Blue pomander**
A STRIKING NEW INTERPRETATION OF A POMANDER

Colour. It stops you in your tracks. A lime-green dress in a shop window, red patent pumps on slender legs, zingy orange marigolds that catch your eye as they spill from a market barrow… A flower shop's aim is to entice you in to purchase those irresistible acid-pink nerines or an armful of glorious tulips that you simply can't do without.

Colour trends come and go. For us, the key to these trends begins on the catwalk. What the fashion designers choose will determine what finds its way on to the high street. I remember when a few years ago, the whole country seemed awash with lilac. It filtered its way into interiors in paint, cushions, bed linen. Brides began to choose lilac and – lo, and behold – several varieties of rose appeared with a lilac hue.

This, of course, is no accident. Growers are now taking advice from trend forecasters – people who predict new colours and trends for the fashion industry – several years in advance. The grower who creates a beautiful flower in a new shade is sure to make a fortune as demand grows. When the East meets West trend hit the streets, the growers were ready. Never-before-seen lime-green spider chrysanths appeared in flower shops, while midori-green carnations changed people's view of the flower as old-fashioned and passé. Green gladioli and ranunculus amazed us, leaving us flower fanatics wondering, whatever next? Well, that is the wonderful thing about flowers. We have our all-time favourites, yet we still hunger for the new, gobble it up and move on to the next bright thing. For me, it is this constant rejuvenation that keeps me coming back for more. It's the fascination that I feel as I look closely at a new bloom – its breathtaking markings, like brush strokes of colour on a fairy wing.

This book breaks down a range of colours into seasons, which I hope will help you enormously with the availability and seasonality of flowers, and also inspire you with the textures and shapes and, possibly most importantly, the mood of the season. Seasonality is difficult to pin down, especially when talking to a global audience. It's now doubly awkward as flower seasons are expanding thanks to improved world transport. Hydrangeas, once typical of late summer and autumn, now appear all year round, flown in from Columbia and Holland. Delicate pink peonies arrive in the UK markets in the chilliest of winters. In their ball gowns of chiffon petals, they seem almost underdressed among robust pine cones and winter chrysanthemums. How dreadful, you may cry – yet imagine the delight of a winter bride, whose vision of her big day means that nothing less than peonies will do.

In this book I take you through the seasons, colour by colour. No matter what the season, you'll find a colour to match your mood. The images are there to inspire, but not to imprison your imagination. Designs can be created in alternative colours and flowers, and in different seasons. Look closely at how I've chosen colours and textures that work together and look good in an inexplicable way. Where I've used containers that might be difficult for you to get hold of, search out your own mismatched teapots, odd shoes, packaging and other vessels. Highlight a beloved painting, frame or prized possession by choosing a bloom that works with the object, picking out colours and hues. Embrace spontaneity – there's a new generation of flowers and colours out there.

Jane Packer

Red

Blood red: the very name evokes a sense of alarm. Red hot, a warning not to touch, yet in today's slang it's a statement of attraction, of sizzling sensuality. Red light, the age-old signal of sex for sale; a red dress can look stunning or sleazy, red lips starlet or harlot. Red is the heart of colour for Christmas, the passionate symbol of Valentine's Day; it adds heat during the summer and as it deepens in autumn, gives a glow that warms the soul on blustery days.

Opposite and below — The parrot tulip is a remarkable beast. I refer to it in that way because, as the flower ages, it matures: the markings expand and the feathery fringed petals appear even more raggedy as the parrot is 'hatched'. I prefer tulips at their full-blown blowsy best to the tight, freshly cut stage. This heart-shaped vase has been filled with 'Topparrot' tulips. I have massed their heads together and nestled crystal brooches among them to reflect the jewel colours of both flowers and vase. Tulip stems continue to grow in the vase: as the stems lengthen, they weaken, so by cutting them short you are allowing the flower heads to be supported by the vase.

The wonderful thing about having red flowers in spring is that they add a little warmth to the day. We may have just experienced a red overload at Christmas but we do need something cheerful on cold frosty mornings. Red flowers will do the trick. I never grow tired of amaryllis, particularly the deep burgundy variety 'Royal Velvet'. And the red, almost black, tulips 'Arma' are just so amazing I'd have armfuls of them all year round if only I could.

Opposite — A vast globe of red glass planted with red primulas. The plants naturally form a dome shape that echoes the vase itself. Fill the vase with scrunched-up polythene to support the plants. Remove the plants from their plastic pots and squeeze them into the mouth of the vase. *Below* — I am a huge fan of packaging – I just had to buy these cola cans! I've filled them with water and put a couple of stems into each opening. The red anemones and ranunculus match the red cans. Lined up, they make a fun image – perfect for a kitchen table.

Opposite and above — This is what I find incredible about flowers: the unbelievable details, the touches of colour that develop in each petal. I love the combination of the aptly named snake's head fritillary with its burgundy flowers and iridescent silver foliage, here mixed with wine-coloured leaves from *Begonia rex* and blood-red velvet gold-laced polyanthus flowers outlined in buttercup yellow. The colours and textures work in perfect harmony. This tied posy has a magical woodland feel. It would suit a dainty spring bride, elfin-like in appearance, or a tiny flower girl.

Project No-bake cake

Here's a three-tiered wedding cake made from three varieties of roses. Well, why not? I've been to so many weddings where the cake goes to waste.

Step 1 — Cut the individual tiers from florist's foam. Before soaking them in water, wrap them in chicken wire so that the 'cakes' don't collapse on their plinths.

Step 2 — Choose roses in shades to tie in with your wedding theme. Cut their stems to approximately 3cm long. To build up each tier, start at the base and add rows of roses, pushing each stem firmly into the foam. Work towards the centre of the tier, leaving space for the pillars.

Step 3 — Add the pillars and carefully balance the tiers on top. Hey presto, your alternative wedding cake!

Summer brings with it a vast
selection of hot red blooms,
from alarm-bell scarlet sweetpeas
to deep beetroot sweet williams.
Red is warming – mix it with polka
dots and you have a strong playful
look. On this page I have assembled
a mixture of red glass tumblers
and goblets and filled each with
a different flower. From left, I've
used astrantia, velvety celosia with
a small tumbler of sweet williams
in the foreground, dappled roses,
sweetpeas with fronds of astilbe
behind, a single dahlia head
and hydrangeas.

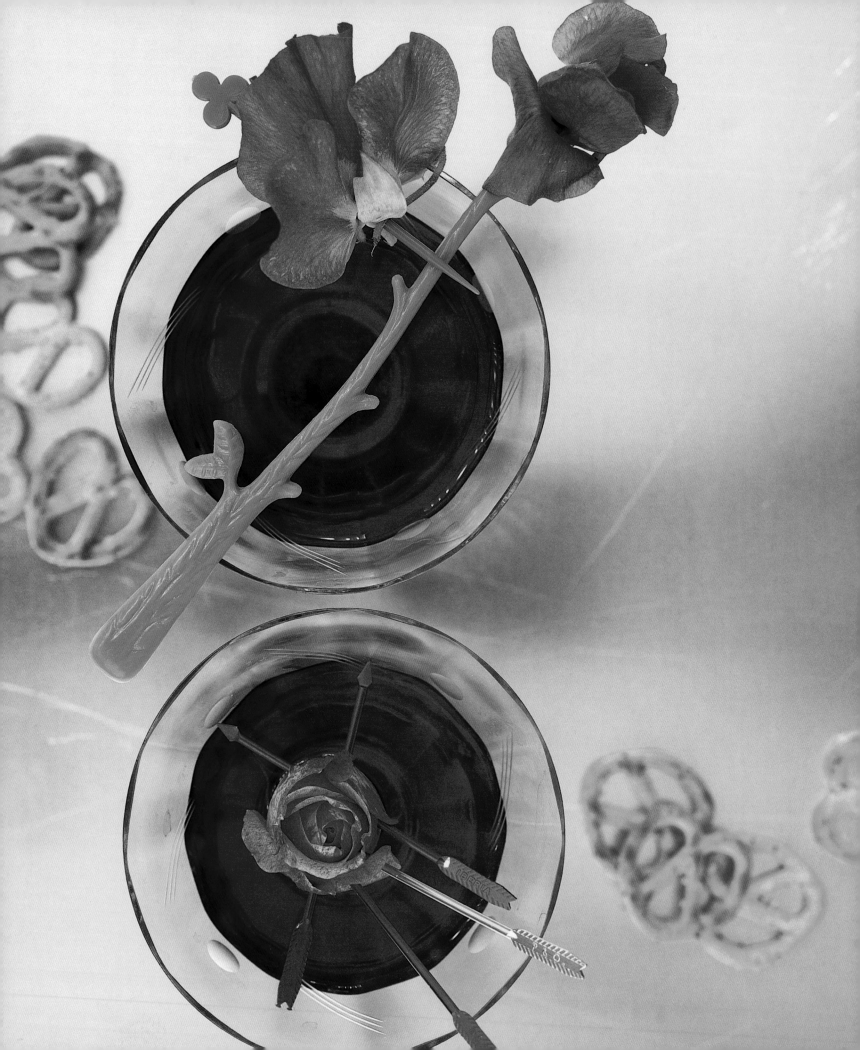

Opposite — In the peak of summer, overload your party. Nothing succeeds like excess! Here I've added a little humour by placing flowers in cocktails. Spear flower heads with cocktail sticks that hold the flower head aloft from the drinks.
Below left — There are now several varieties of this red-and-white dappled rose including 'Soutine' and 'Intuition'. I think these are spectacular en masse or mixed with different coloured roses for a true rose-garden image.
Below right—The deeper, darker shades of sweetpeas are stunning. Ketchup red mixed with deep violet purple and burgundy are intense.

Red in summer says heat, so if you're after a tropical statement red flowers will lend a hand. Red roses are a favourite of mine, particularly 'Black Baccara'. I love their deep velvety sheen. I suppose you could say summer is the perfect time for roses, although with imported flowers from Columbia and Ecuador, we can buy great-quality roses with huge flower heads all year round. But what these flowers tend to lack is scent. Red roses tend to be highly scented – sweet and musky, too. Their perfume transports me back to childhood: I want to run from bloom to bloom, throwing petals into the air.

 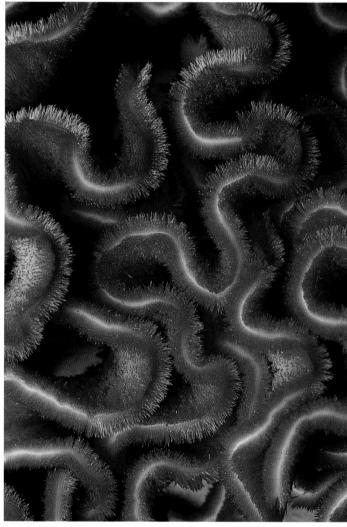

Above left — This red mahogany-coloured bamboo is fantastic. It's available all year round and makes a great support for plants or weak-stemmed flowers.

Above right — Amazing celosia! It's just like crushed velvet. Most people think it's quite an ugly flower, but I love the weirdness of its texture. Although it arrives on long stems, I prefer to cut them short, using the soft 'fabric' of the flower at low level, with smaller flowers peering above.

Opposite — Tiny pieces of kalanchoe lined up in miniature glass bottles make a great table centrepiece. I am quite into these tiny vases at the moment and think that their impact is huge, despite their size. The key is to use lots.

Project Pedestal arrangement

This pedestal arrangement is a cornucopia of colour, but with a definite leaning towards red. Dark burgundy copper beech foliage outlines the shape, with blocks of velvety scarlet celosia towards the centre mixed with deep red peonies. Purple aster, stocks and delphiniums are grouped with yellow solidago, eremurus and sunflowers. The amber tones in the centre come from melon flesh and pineapple!

Step 1 — Fill an urn with florist's foam and cover with chicken wire. The chicken wire helps to hold the foam together, vital when so many stems are being used.

Step 2 — Start to build the outline shape with the foliage, beginning at the back. Next add the tallest stems, such as eremurus.

Step 3 — Insert flowers in groups of four or five stems at a time.

Step 4 — Place the pineapple in the centre of the arrangement. Do this by pushing the fruit on to a sharp cane and inserting the cane into the foam.

Step 5 — Rip open the melon with a knife and push a cane into the fruit. Then use the cane to hold the melon in the foam.

Step 6 — Use flowers to fill in the shape: the corners, centre and front overhang. To get the right shape at the front, push the stems upwards into the foam, from below the top of the urn.

A bicycle covered in cotoneaster berries, which have been wired to the frame using reel wire, as have the roses on the mudguard. The basket has been filled with 'Grand Prix' roses and tumbling strands of celosia. I can just imagine a design like this propped against a wall at a village fête, a wedding or some other kind of celebration.

Below — Dark red celosia is available through the summer months and is at its best from July to early September. These tassels of crushed-velvet blossoms are so dramatic: they are very flexible and grow approximately 30cm/12in long. They are also available in a faded sage green. I love this flower, as it is so useful for pedestal arrangements, tumbling down over the edge of containers. It looks great in a tall vase: you really get to see its full beauty and drama. It's fantastic for wedding bouquets; I included it in mine and loved the theatrical element. Although there are lots of other trailing ingredients, such as clematis, jasmine and stephanotis, there's nothing quite like celosia.

Autumn has to be the best season for red and its adjacent tones as leaves change colour from green to shades of red, burgundy, amber and orange. Photinia has wonderful glossy red leaves, cotoneaster has vivid orange-red berries, cotinus foliage has hints of deep purple, while, stripped of their leaves, the slender red branches of Cornus alba are perfect for displaying in vases or twisting into wreaths. There is a definite smell to autumn: the tang of bonfires as gardens are cleared for winter; and the strong almost herbal scent of chrysanthemums — it's pungent, yet I love it.

Opposite — Do you remember as a child using berries and fruit like make-up to stain your lips and cheeks? And dressing up in your mother's old clothes, tripping over as you scraped along in noisy high heels? Well, I couldn't help thinking of this when I was putting together a headdress of these glorious 'Classy' roses, fruits and berries. The roses, celosia, grapes and redcurrants have been wired on to a circlet of wire that fits the model's head.

Above — Fruits like these jewel-bright translucent redcurrants mix easily with flowers in all sorts of arrangements.

This still-life includes a branching stem of *Ilex verticillata* berries, 'Red Intuition' dark red roses, a red slipper orchid (in the centre), a multiheaded stem of orchids (in the foreground), an anemone and a red gerbera – all available in the winter months. Red flowers demand a premium price at peak periods like Christmas and Valentine's Day. Wonderful as they are for these occasions, you may want to think about varying your theme and going for a frosty winter white at Christmas or a hot pink for Valentine's Day. You'll certainly get more for your money if you do.

Opposite — I love the triumphant flowers of amaryllis, held aloft on a thick, tubular stem. But one drawback is that the heavy bloom can become too much for the stem. To support it, try inserting a cane into the entire length of the stem.

Below left — Orangey-red leucospermum look almost artificial, with 'plastic' tendrils surrounding a centre that resembles a spider's web. The heads are supported on rigid woody stems; they dry easily and will last an age.

Below right — These red anemones are fully open, showing their black centres. I like to buy them closed and watch them unfurl.

Typical red blooms in winter will include anemone, gerbera, cymbidium orchid, slipper orchid, ilex, 'Grand Prix' rose and 'Black Magic' rose. The red gerbera is quite readily obtainable in a different size (germini), numerous other shades of red and with different petal formations. And, just as you tire of one, it seems another is developed: pimpernel, timo, ferrari and explosion are all interesting shapes, colours and textures. Roses such as the magnificent 'Grand Prix' have an enormous head size and lifespan, holding their velvety petals for anything up to two weeks and beyond when kept in the right conditions. 'Black Magic' is a smaller headed rose but with a glorious depth of colour. The bright red glossy berried branches of ilex are only available in the winter months, somehow I feel making it more special. The anemone with its naïve, child-like shape is delicately beautiful in its form.

Right — The dogwood in this vase has been employed in a dramatic way. Some of the colourful stems have been cut to the width of the vase and float horizontally on the surface of the water, while others have been left longer to criss-cross. For maximum impact stand it alongside another vase of red flowers. (Dogwood is also available in lime green.)

Opposite — This cake of 'Grand Prix' roses and dogwood makes a beautiful centrepiece. Cut the shape from florist's foam, soak it in water, then pin the pieces of dogwood around the outside, using the ribbon to hide the pins. Then push the rose stems into the foam. You can use an alternative to roses, but always choose flat-topped flowers to create an even surface. Instead of dogwood, try using coloured leaves such as pussy willow or cherry blossom.

Project Berry wreath

The wreath is a symbol of eternity, the neverending circle of life, which is why they are used for both funerals and as circlets of flowers on the heads of brides and bridesmaids. In many countries the wreaths are used to decorate homes throughout the seasons and not simply over the festive period, which is a tradition I love.

Step 1 — Buy a circular wreath frame from a florist's or garden centre, and bind it on to a reel of florist's wire.

Step 2 — Cut the stems of ilex berries into lengths of around 15cm/6in and bind them on to the stem with florist's wire. Working in a clockwise direction, add more and more stems as you rotate the frame, making sure you distance each stem approximately 7cm/3in from the last and that you cover the cut ends with the berried pieces as you go.

Step 3 — Continue until both ends meet. Cut off the wire. You can add a bow if you desire. This will last a month on an outside door in a cool climate; inside, the berries will shrivel but will not drop.

White

White exudes serenity and sophistication. It is cool and breathtaking, and casts a gentle, diffused light. And it's not just a single tone: there is an entire spectrum of whites. In Victorian times the hothouses of grand homes would be filled with deliciously fragrant blooms of pure white waxy gardenias and stephanotis. Many famous style gurus have cited white flowers as their favourite blooms – Coco Chanel, Christian Dior and Guccio Gucci to name but a few.

Opposite — I've used branches of green-white cherry blossom in a hedge-like manner, filling several creamy-white oblong ceramic vases against a silvery background. Branches from a garden would be thick and gnarled; grown commercially (in Italy) they are thinner and more pliable. Stems arrive around a metre in length, so I've cut them shorter.

Below — Cherry blossom is much prized in Japan and cherry blossom season is celebrated everywhere. News bulletins on TV track the blossom's progress and streets are decorated with artificial branches attached to lamp posts. People picnic in parks beneath the canopy of blossom, and visit temples and shrines to enjoy the trees.

As the seasons change, so do the flowers we desire. These days many flowers have their seasons extended by commercial growers so they are available throughout the year. Don't get me wrong: I am delighted that beautiful heads of hydrangea are around for 12 months, but it somehow makes things like white narcissi in spring all the more precious. I love the scent of spring. When you walk into the flower market while the narcissi season is at its peak, the scent is overwhelming. Paperwhites are my favourite variety, particularly the long-stemmed ones. Add to that white parrot tulips, white blossom and white amaryllis and I am in white-flower heaven.

Opposite — Christian Dior wore lily of the valley as a daily buttonhole. It flowers naturally in May, in time for Labour Day in France, when it is traditionally sold on street corners. Forced in glasshouses out of season for bridal bouquets, the stems are much finer, elongated and paler in colour.

This page — The delicate paperwhite narcissus is another typical spring flower and gloriously scented. These tiny star-shaped flowers have been removed from their stems and stitched to bridal slippers. It's not a longlasting decoration, but it's absolutely charming. For sturdier flowers substitute white dendrobium orchids.

Opposite and above — Snowdrops, so pure and delicate in appearance, are tough little devils, poking their heads through a blanket of snow. They have short stems, so are best used in small bunches and make a delightful gift wrapped in a scrap of pretty paper. A perfect example of less is more.

Opposite — The serrated edges of these white tulips are amazingly similar to the feathered wings of swans. These retro containers have been filled with flowers only – any green foliage would detract from the snowy-white feathery petals.

Below — When you look close up, the detail of flower and foliage never ceases to amaze me. Like soft furry grey mice, the flowers of pussy willow (*Salix caprea*) are followed by unfurling green leaves.

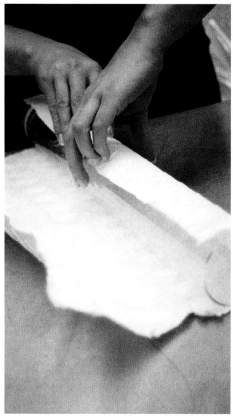
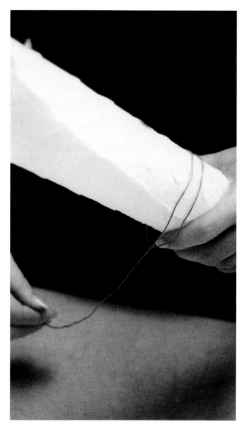

Project All wrapped up

Wrapping these tall vases in textured white paper and binding them with green twine matches the white and green of the narcissi they hold. The stems are bound tightly together so they fit snugly in the vase, giving an illusion of enormous length when the stems in fact finish just halfway down.

Step 1 — Wrap the empty vases in textured paper – I've used handmade Japanese paper – and secure with twine three-quarters of the way up.

Step 2 — Gather the narcissi in one hand and bind them just below the flower heads with string. Let the leaves stand naturally. Trim the stems so the base of the bunch is even. Weight the bases of the vases with pebbles to stop them toppling, then fill with water and add the flowers.

Opposite — This peony arrangement has more than 50 stems massed into a dome, so it's expensive to produce. For a cheaper alternative use white chrysanthemums, carnations or hydrangeas. Pack an urn with a block of wet florist's foam and start by creating a complete arc of flowers from one side of the urn to the other, making sure the flower lengths are even, then fill in the gaps. The fact that no foliage is included creates a more modern look and intensifies the colour and simplicity of the arrangement.

Below — This close-up is the tip of a white eremurus or foxtail lily. The flowers open from the bottom of the flower head upwards, so trim the lower ones as they die off to extend the appeal of the flower.

There's one thing that white flower borders in summer have the edge over on spring – warmth. I am very much a sun-loving creature; I love the feeling of sun on my skin. Imagine a warm day, green grass to sit on and white daisies surrounding you – wonderful! When I think of tall spires of white delphinium, bees humming around sweet-scented white lilies, I am transported to a sunny place. I have to admit that peonies are one of my favourite flowers. I adore their layer-upon-layer of chiffon petals and their delicate perfume that lingers in the air. The flowers open quickly so buy them in tight bud.

White hydrangeas are like heavenly clouds. And they are so versatile: you can mass the heads together to create a dome of flowers or use them separately. I have no problem with people buying a single bloom from my store; quite often with modern vases, a single stem is all that's required – and I've always been an advocate of 'less is more'. For a rustic feel, on this page I've used natural containers that would look great on the floor in front of a fireplace. The pale bark of the silver birch logs works so well with the white hydrangea heads. The logs have been drilled in the centre to hold test tubes filled with water to keep the flowers fresh. The heavy blooms sit flat on top of the logs, with no stem showing.

Project Dressed in flowers

Every so often the chance to create something whimsical comes along, perhaps for a wedding or a party. As a business we've received commissions for a Midsummer Night's Dream party and a Mad Miss Havisham haunt, complete with ripped muslin, over-grown ivy and theatrical cobwebs. Working on film sets has given us the opportunity to design bouquets for movies such as *Alfie* and *Love Actually*. Here I've made a skirt of mixed summer flowers using chicken wire as a base. This was for a one-off, stationary photograph – if you intend the skirt to be worn, I suggest you make it from fabric and stitch on faux flowers to make it a lot more comfortable, as well as longer lasting.

Step 1 — Choose the flowers. I've used peonies, larkspur, delphinium, phlox and lysimachia.
Step 2 — Gather them in small bunches and bind them together with wire.
Step 3 — Stitch them firmly on to the skirt with the taller spires of flower heads hanging downwards.

I've used an amazing pale turquoise pumpkin for the arrangement pictured here. It looks as though it's made from jade porcelain. I've topped it with this mad spidery-looking grey air plant – so weird in itself that it's sure to be a conversation piece. The texture of the air plant is dusty, almost artificial, with leaves forming a rosette-like centre. Air plants are part of the bromeliad family and they are just like they sound – plants that survive on moisture from the atmosphere. The colour match between the cyclamen leaves, pumpkin and air plant is what makes this combination work and my heart sing! I have hollowed out a few miniature white pumpkins and filled them with water to hold the white cyclamen flowers and their beautiful leaves.

White is not a colour that automatically springs to mind when we think of autumn. We tend to lean towards the obvious bronzes and golds of the season. But think of white chrysanthemum blooms with their herbal scent, of honesty seed pods (sometimes called silver dollars), with their outer casing stripped away to reveal the translucent white lining, and of white pumpkins. They all suggest to me a bright, fresh, crisp morning, with spider webs outlined in frost and shining in the early sunlight.

Project Autumn wreath

Wreaths can be used for every season. Miniature 'Tête-à-Tête' narcissi left on the bulb are great for creating a wreath to celebrate spring. A summer symbol of roses, hydrangea, jasmine and peonies could be hung at the gates of a wedding ceremony. Here I've made a circle of oak leaves and perry pears for autumn – simple yet apt. I have washed the finished decoration with a light touch of white paint to create an autumn frost. To make a wreath with heavy ingredients like fruit, the old-fashioned moss and wire frame method is best – if you don't want pears tumbling every time someone slams the door. For fresh flowers use a wreath made of florist's foam.

Step 1 — Buy a circular wreath frame (or make your own). Bind the moss to the frame using string or wire, making sure

you have used enough to hold heavy items like the pears in place.

Step 2 — Push a strong florist's wire horizontally through a pear.

Step 3 — Push another vertically through the fruit from base to stem, making a cross through the fruit. Twist the wires together behind the pear (you'll use them to attach the fruit to the frame).

Step 4 — Make small bunches of foliage and bind the stems together with wire, leaving two long 'legs' of wire to attach the bunch to the frame.

Step 5 — Push the wires through the mossed frame, twisting to fasten fruit or foliage in place and tucking the ends back into the moss to conceal them.

Step 6 — Spray gently with white aerosol paint to add a light dusting for a frosty effect.

White cotton buds on chocolate-brown stems, perfectly pure snowdrops, star-shaped Christmas roses and majestic white amaryllis are all winter flowers I look forward to, not to mention the greyish, chalky-white eucalyptus buds and grevillea foliage, all worth getting cold feet and a red nose for! White flowers have an air of sophistication and I have many customers who will order nothing else – it's just as well there's plenty to choose from even in the depths of winter. On the shorter side there are anemones, freesia, narcissi, ranunculus, chincherinchee. For medium and tall vases there are lilies, orchids, chrysanthemums, various blossoms, peonies, roses and hydrangeas, all in varying tones of white.

Opposite — The first flower is chincherinchee: long shiny stems support a cone-shaped flower head with a few white star-like flowers open at the base. The flowers gradually open all the way up the cone. Next is a variety of blossom that is available in early January, with delicate buds that open along the stem. Then comes white narcissi. There are many different varieties and their tiny star-like flowers emit an incredible perfume. White phalaenopsis or moth orchids have a fleshy textured flower that opens slowly and lasts for a month or more. Chrysanthemum blooms are available in many shapes and colours. I prefer this flower head, which curves in towards the centre, but has petals at the edge that curl back. Ranunculus is one of my absolute favourite flowers, with layer upon layer of fragile petals. The arum lily is a cone of fleshy petal that curves around a thick central spadix. This graceful flower is simplicity itself, yet speaks of exclusivity and style.

Opposite — So often when creating a large arrangement for an event, I search for something a little more alternative to the traditional triangular pedestal arrangement. For me, this Sixties shop display stand is perfect. I've refilled it with a mix of white flowers (roses, dahlias, hydrangeas, eucharis and chrysanthemums) plus white pumpkins. As it's a temporary display for one night these flowers will survive without water.

Above — No matter how many vases you own, sometimes you still can't find the right one for the arrangement you have in mind. One solution is to use a glass cube vase as I've done here. I've covered it with a piece of silver leather and filled it with bunches of white ranunculus. The flowers have simply been trimmed to size and allowed to fall naturally over the sides.

Above — This large white rose looks as though it has been cut from the garden. In fact it's a commercially grown bloom that has been artfully tweaked. By plucking a few of the petals from the centre to reveal the golden yellow stamens, the effect is changed from a long-stemmed glamorous white rose to a full, open garden bloom. This is a professional trick we use when we need that softer, natural look.

Opposite — In the cold months of winter, these glorious creatures unfurl from a cluster of thick shiny leaves and the flower unfolds to this perfect white star. It's held on a fleshy brown stem similar to that of a cyclamen. They are not roses of course, but hellebores (*Helleborus niger*).

Green

Green is the very lifeblood of nature, but we still tend to associate the colour with foliage rather than flowers. This is all starting to change: over the past decade some extraordinary green flowers have come on to the market and I'm still reeling with amazement. Green has single-handedly reinvented the chrysanthemum and the much-maligned carnation, reinstating them as desirable fashion flowers. Roses, anthurium and ranunculus have benefited from this infusion of green, too. Add to them the older generation of green-tinted arum lilies, gladioli, hydrangeas, euphorbias and hellebores and you've got an unbelievable palette of green flowers.

Fresh, lush green: there's nothing like the first green spears of daffodils, as the grey mist of winter lifts and the light changes to that stark, bright spring sunlight. Trees burst with green as buds swell and leaves unfurl. If it's the middle of winter and you're impatient for spring, don't despair! You can still inject the mood that fresh green can bring. A green vase of white flowers will do the trick, or branches painted luminous green, water tinted with specialist florist's dyes or food colouring, or pots of houseplants topped with green pebbles or gravel.

Opposite — From left, I've set a green hellebore in a lime-green bowl with green glass chippings. In front, a rack of test tubes holds heads of fountain grass (*Panicum*). There's a dark green glass bottle with a small posy of *Alchemilla mollis*, and a bright lime-green vase holds soft heads of guelder roses. From there, a tall clear green vase holds a branch that I painted luminous green. There's a bowl of budding daffodils with green chippings to hide the soil, while a transparent green plastic bowl holds hyacinths in their early stages. Ornamental cabbage heads have been cut from their long stems and massed into a bowl of intense acid green. Just in front sits another green hellebore. The large spears at the back are agave succulents.

Above — A remarkable close-up of a green ranunculus. I love ranunculus anyway, but the green version is completely different. The petals are short and crimped, and curl inwards.

Opposite — A black glass urn holds widow iris and green ranunculus. The widow iris is so called because of its black velvety petals that cloak a green throat. The flowers have a very short lifespan, which makes them an unlikely commercial venture. But for just a few weeks of the year I can find a couple of precious boxes in Covent Garden. Beneath the urn I've placed an auricula, a type of primula. I've chosen one that has black petals to coordinate with the vase and irises above.

Opposite — To exaggerate a green theme, I spray-painted an urn Day-glo green. I kept the stems of the arum lilies as long and straight as possible. They are held together beneath the flower heads with Perspex straws that match the colour of the urn. Twists of wire keep the straws in place – the luminous green ribbons hide the wire. At the base of the stems I've used heads of fountain grass (*Panicum*) as an alternative to moss.

Above left — Spring euphorbia: I love it! It really brightens the garden early in the season. It's available commercially, although not on a great scale. Take care when using it, as the milky sap that leaks from the cut stems can irritate the skin.

Above right — A green hellebore close up to show you its delicate brush-stroke markings.

A change of green for the change of season. This gathering of flower heads has a late summer/early autumn harvest feel. From left, in the first green vase I have placed large dark glossy hydrangea leaves (hydrangea is now sold as a cut foliage, as well as a flower) and tucked a large thistle head in with them. In the next vase a single sunflower that has had its yellow petals removed gains a second lease of life: the petal-less head is interesting enough to be used in its naked state. Then comes an ornamental brassica or cabbage, with the stem cut short. Side shoots from a delphinium have been mixed with variegated grass, and finally there's a silvery grey poppy head.

Opposite and below — The wooden
figure hugs a large poppy head. Unlike
the poppy head below, it has an
incredible ruffled collar. We call this
variety 'Hen and Chicks', because the
head looks like a hen with her chicks
gathered round. I love seed heads as

an ingredient in a bouquet – they're
not beautiful in the pretty sense but
interesting in texture. I like to add that
surprise element to a Jane Packer
bouquet and to watch its effect: the
recipient astonished by flowers and
foliage they've never seen before.

The excitement as a warm breeze ripples the green landscape,
blowing through trees and green wheat in the fields before the
sun truly ripens it. Vegetables on allotments; market stalls piled
high with apples, gooseberries, greengages; the lawns that
English men take so seriously – an aerial view of England in
summer is like a green patchwork that makes my heart sing. My
own garden is very green, broken with only a touch of colour.
And even these have a green stage. The greyish-green furry
case of the poppy flower before it bursts open to reveal its
crumpled petals; tight green buds with their promise of what's
to come – be it a rose, lily or peony.

Project Green globe

I'm not sure if you can gauge the height of these hydrangeas and trailing amaranthus, but it is rather grand. At more than a metre tall it is suitable for a dinner table, as its shape will not restrict a view across the table.

Step 1 — Put water in the vase and twirl some grass into the water. Add florist's dyes or food colouring for extra interest. Pebbles or gravel would have the same effect.

Step 2 — Place a bowl in the top of the vase. Fix it in place with fix gum (strong florist's gum) and strap the presoaked foam into the bowl with florist's tape.

Step 3 — Push the hydrangea stems into the foam to create a dome. Start at the base, angling the stem upwards so the head hides the bowl and the foam.

Step 4 — Add the trails of green amaranthus.

Opposite and below — Close up to the rose 'Illusion' you can see its wonderful variation in colour. I believe it was given its name because its open flowers give the impression of an older full-blown rose. Unlike most roses for the cut-flower trade, the flowers of 'Illusion' are left growing on the bush until they open, then they are cut and sent to market. I've mixed them with those wonderful winter cabbage leaves that have a bluish-green bloom, arranged in florist's foam within a green trug. A new take on the expression cabbage rose.

The last of the green leaves become so precious in autumn before they change colour and fall from the trees, whirling and floating in the breeze. Autumn also means leafy green vegetables and harvest time, celebrating the season with dried foliage arrangements for our homes. Now, of course, we have a fantastic selection of green flowers to add to our displays: carnations, chrysanthemums, zinnias and tropical green anthuriums. I don't like to mix tropical flowers with the more garden-like ingredients, especially as there is a whole range of wonderful tropical green foliage available all year round, such as huge, deeply cut monstera leaves, shiny aspidistra and fatsia leaves lobed like green hands.

Above left — To display these ornamental apples try setting a small clear glass vase within a larger one, making sure there is room to 'pour' the apples into the gap between. Alternatively, they can be wired on to false stems and used in bouquets. Use the same technique as for wiring the pears in the wreath on page 66, then bind the apple on to a small cane or discarded flower stem.

Above right — When using cabbage leaves in an arrangement (see previous page), you need to strip away a little of the leaf (about 2cm/¾in) at the base, leaving just the central vein. Cut that at a sharp angle, so it pushes easily into florist's foam.

Opposite — This versatile garland of steel grass and slipper orchids could hang at the entrance to a wedding or wrap round a large vase.

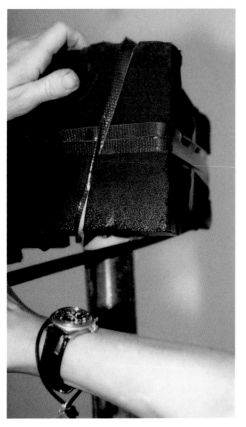

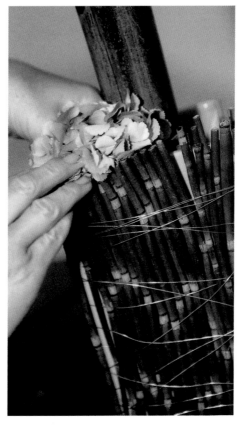

Project Topiary tree

This topiary of green ingredients almost disappears into the trompe-l'oeil background, making this a three-dimensional scene. For a special occasion create several 'trees', varying their height and the flowers you use, making some floor-standing, plus smaller versions for table decorations.

Step 1 — Choose a tall rectangular container. Fix a bamboo post by pushing it down into a large block of presoaked florist's foam that will fit into your container. Then bind blocks of wet florist's foam on to the upper part of the stem with florist's tape.

Step 2 — Cut the sunflowers' stems at a sharp angle and push them into the foam.

Step 3 — Cover the container with strands of snake grass, binding them in place with green wire. If you can't get snake grass, large glossy leaves like aspidistra are a good alternative.

Step 4 — Fill the gap between the post and the rim of the container with moss or another green ingredient – I've used hydrangea flowers.

The bento boxes (Japanese lunch boxes) on this page are filled with flowers to make a fun alternative to a traditional table centre – even better if there is an oriental theme to the occasion. They can be made with flowers of any colour – pink at cherry blossom time would be perfect. First, place a thin slice of wet florist's foam in the bottom of the box. Then make the snakegrass grid by binding it with wire, string, leather, shoelaces – anything that looks good. Then place a flower or fruit in each section. If one flower doesn't fill the space, try several grouped together, just as food would be grouped and presented in a Japanese restaurant.

Opposite — Ten green bottles… Well, six actually – different plastic household bottles that I painted green. This is my way of recycling! In the bottles I've used green skimmia and catkins in their tight stage before they open into yellow tassels. The bottom right-hand bottle holds thick magnolia leaves with brown suede undersides. *Below left* — 'Green Wonder' chrysanthemums look like sea anemones close up. *Below right* — Skimmia blossom is perfect for wedding bouquets, as the foliage holds its moisture and will not wilt.

Foliage is an important ingredient at any time of the year but never more so than at Christmas. It's vital for traditional wreaths and garlands: shiny laurel, magnolia leaves with undersides like brown suede, holly and, of course, pine with its delicious scent. The scent of a Christmas tree is imprinted on our memory from childhood – the excitement of buying the tree, decorating it with favourite trimmings each year. I still love that sense of nostalgia as I pull out the favourite decorations from their box. My children always have a small tree in their rooms that acts as a sort of Advent calendar. Even my dog, Ted, had his own Advent-calendar tree one year. Not such a good idea… he ate all the treats hanging from it in one night and was promptly sick!

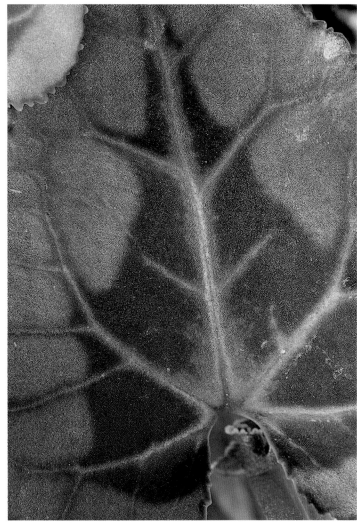

Above left — I like these branches covered in lichen. Try tying small bunches together with raffia and use them to decorate planted baskets. Lichen or reindeer moss grows in damp woodlands. It's soft and grey and dries to a brittle state; or you can buy it treated with glycerine to keep it pliable.

Above right — A real close-up of a cyclamen leaf. Just look at the amazing markings and beautiful colouring. It's as if fairies have been out during the night painting them. This is another great foliage to use in wired wedding work, as the fleshy leaf holds moisture and won't collapse during the day.

Opposite — Single parrot tulips held in place by diamanté brooches. White parrot tulips begin their life with strong green markings.

Yellow

Warm and mellow as dappled sunshine or sharp as a lemon, yellow can be welcoming and heart-warming but, equally, it can be bright, brash and sharp. Yellow is enchanting: it's laughter as you pick buttercups, the delight of a fluffy newly hatched chick, fields of Aztec sunflowers that follow the warmth of the sun. Yet the Victorians named a yellow rose 'Jealousy'. Is there a side to yellow that we should be wary of – or is it sunshine in a vase?

The array of spring flowers pictured here – all in shades of warm yellow – gives an idea of what's around during this season. Starting from the left, we have two small heads of gold-laced polyanthus tucked in beside the stem of a yellow arum. Then comes an orange ranunculus and a yellow variety disappearing off the page. Low down is a tulip – a very obvious spring flower available in all kinds of colours and shapes. The final three groupings are narcissi: there are literally dozens of different varieties available, ranging from the tiny multiheaded yellow 'Tête-à-tête' (on the far right) to the huge-bloomed traditional yellow daffodil 'Dutch Master'. The yellow-and-white ones are 'Ice Follies'. A lesser-known variety but one of my favourites (though not pictured here) is 'Bridal Crown', which has soft cream button-shaped flowers, multiheaded, with a milder spring fragrance. Keep narcissi in cool water and a cool position for longer life: they are delicate creatures but oh so worthy of the extra care.

Below left — A gold-laced polyanthus flower edged in pure yellow. It's a member of the primrose family, which includes hundreds of varieties. With its dark colouring and unusual edging, it's similar to my favourites – auriculas.
Below right — Ranunculus are available in many colours and shades. They belong to the buttercup family but happen to have lots more petals, curled into a tight bud that gradually unfurls into this beautiful flower.
Opposite — Shades of gold, from the pure waxy cones of arum lilies and new breed of yellow hyacinth, to the cheerful rancunculus, narcissi and polyanthus and a single cymbidium orchid floating in a jelly glass.

What I love about yellow flowers in spring is their sense of newness. The bright sharp yellows seem freshly painted – to symbolize a new beginning, a new year. I love their intense colour and their scent. Hyacinths on the bulb are a particular favourite of mine and now there is a new arrival, with yellow blooms to back up the other shades of blue, pink and white. Their scent can be overwhelming in a small room but is perfect for a spring party. I've always claimed that yellow blooms were not my favourite and yet now I realize the sight and smell of yellow flowers in spring – from the dainty primrose to the tall fritillaria – fill me with excitement.

Opposite — A single orchid, bright neon yellow floating in a glass bowl of the same colour, can be so powerful! The single daffodil, simply presented in a yellow teacup, is beautiful in its quiet simplicity. A tiny gathering of primrose and 'Tête-à-Tête' narcissi is small and precious, when given by a child. Less is, so often, more.

Above — A fun way to wake someone, replacing their breakfast eggs with ranunculus flowers in shades of egg-yolk yellow. The eggshells hold a little water to keep the flowers fresh.

Project Tulip bowl

These huge-headed, long-stemmed French tulips are incredible. Use them in a way that shows off their assets

Step 1 — Trim all lower stems, ensuring they are clean of soil and tatty leaves.

Step 2 — Use stems that are soft and flaccid so they will bend easily. (Leave out of water for a couple of hours.) Place the stems around the inside of a large goldfish bowl.

Step 3 — Bunch together the remaining stems and trim.

Step 4 — Place the tulips in the bowl, allowing the stems to stand upright as well as bending beautifully over the edge. (You could also make a smaller version using regular-size tulips.)

Yellow arums, gerberas and centaurea thistles in three different gold vessels. The 'vase' on the far left holding the arums is actually a waterproof padded foil envelope – perfect for pinning to an office wall. The yellow gerberas in the central vase have been cut short so that they sit low, with the flower heads resting on the rim to create a low dome. The centaurea are true summer flowers available only for a very short season.

Summer is my favourite season. I love to wake early to the birds singing and the sun rising, promising a warm sunny day. For me, yellow flowers are best when mixed with other bright colours – oranges, reds and pinks. I'm lucky enough to have a small cottage in the wilds of Suffolk where yellow flowers grow wild in the hedgerows. Then there are cottages near by that sell their spare garden flowers. These little mixed bunches are so charming – you leave your money in a tin at the gate and carry your purchases home. I love this look: it's so different from sophisticated city flowers and very close to my heart.

This summer I sat by a field of sunflowers; the sky was blue and swallows
swooped and dived. I couldn't help but feel an overwhelming sense of happiness
and contentment. When I first opened my shop in central London, I would buy
sunflowers from a farmer. They would look marvellous for a day, then sadly hang
their heads and wilt. Now we can buy them easily throughout the year and they
last much longer. These are classic sunflowers but there are quite a few different
varieties to choose from, including flowers with petals of chocolate brown.

Above — This shallow copper plate has enough of a rim to allow a little water to sit in it. You need to look down on a display like this, so use it at a low level. The arrangement has a Moroccan feel, but I've moved on from simply sprinkling petals and used whole heads of marigolds and dahlias, snipped from their stems and floated in the water. The vibrant flowers surround an 'eye' outlined with astrantia flower heads – the pupil is a small sunflower. flower that lasts.

Opposite — When designing flowers for a party or event, I'm always searching for new ideas to decorate tables. This is a quirky arrangement of spray-painted yellow branches supporting lampshades above a mound of citrus gerbera, arum lilies and centaurea. I've included the cable and plug as a joke!

Opposite — I absolutely love peonies. I think they have to be my favourite flowers. There are many varieties that you can grow in the garden, but very few are available from commercial growers in Europe – a great shame, as some are breathtakingly beautiful. I have sprayed a classic shopping basket citrus-orange and filled it with a container of wet florist's foam. Into the foam I've inserted the stems of what I can only describe as jaw-dropping peonies in shades of cream, lemon and apricot. Just look at the size of them! I love the powdery golden-yellow stamens at their heart, which you can see in the close-up above.

117 | *Yellow in summer*

A field of glowing pumpkins is a strange yet wonderful sight. It's almost as if Martians have landed and left behind their alien pods. For this arrangement I've mixed these comical vegetables with orange glass globes, the smallest of which holds burnt-orange brush-like banksias from Australia. Two more vases hold 'Milva' orange roses and a large bowl of shaggy-headed chrysanthemum blooms completes the picture.

Opposite — This extraordinary pumpkin-inspired pram made me laugh – can you imagine pushing your baby around in it! It's a great prop for a window display at Halloween or harvest time. I've filled it with pumpkins and gourds of all shapes and sizes, each with its own individual colouring and markings.

Below — Gourds are ornamental, not edible, and will dry out naturally if left to their own devices. If you hollow out pumpkins to make lanterns at Halloween, don't forget to try to save the flesh – there are hundreds of recipes for pumpkin pies and soups and other dishes, and you can roast the seeds, too.

Autumn is the perfect time for yellow flowers and the colours that fall either side of yellow in the spectrum. Think harvest festival, think golden wheat, chrysanthemums and bronze foliage. Rudbeckia is a daisy-like flower, available only in autumn; so, too, is solidago or golden rod – a fluffy-looking flower that I've used touches of in the large pedestal on page 30. Then there are glowing orange and gold pumpkins and squashes that will last for weeks, lighting up a windowsill or table. We can add to this palette with the all-year-round yellows – sunflowers, lilies and roses – to create a blaze of sunshine before winter sets in.

Below left — These parrot tulips open to a huge bloom, revealing a centre of black stamens. At one time tulips were spring flowers only, but now they appear throughout the year. So here they are sitting next to a creamy poinsettia, a traditional Christmas plant.

Below right — Poinsettias come in many different colours, from bright white and apricot to deep red. They are used mainly as pot plants, although you can buy them as cut stems. Be careful with the cut flower, as the white sap that leaks from the stems can be an irritant.

Daffodils that arrived for Christmas were once a speciality; now we take it for granted that they appear in November and are often around until May. Craspedia is a strange flower, like little cheese balls that are handed out at children's party. They are suspended on very fine stems. There is no need to put these flowers into water, as they dry almost immediately keeping their colour superbly. They are in fact available all year round, but are perfect to add to the winter list of ingredients. Forsythia's, tiny star-like flowers appear when we need them most. Cold winter mornings, barren gardens, naked of greenery… then suddenly they appear like branches of tiny Christmas lights in the darkness. Use in tall vases alone or mixed with lilies or gladioli.

Opposite — A birdcage, a single stem of forsythia and a golden bird. A touch of whimsy that would work brilliantly for a party. Birdcages can be found in junk shops for reasonable prices. At other times of the year twine jasmine or honeysuckle over the top of the cage, with the flowers displayed inside.

Below — Craspedia is strange flower. It looks like a large hatpin and dries really easily. The strange flowers look like pompoms or little cheese balls. It can be difficult to work with as the stems are so rigid and leafless, so I've tied them together with the heads massed and displayed with the two bunches opposite one another in a shallow vase.

125 | *Yellow in winter*

Pink

Pink is the colour of femininity: soft, warm and inviting. It's young, fun and fresh. Pink means peonies, ranunculus and roses – all of them flowers with layers of personality and sensuality and petals that sweep and sashay like the flounciest ballgowns. One of my dreams is to visit Morocco and see the mountains of pink rose petals harvested for their intense fragrance and crushed for their expensive, precious oil.

I've used spring flowers in the ultimate girly way by making the necklace of pink hyacinth florets pictured here. I used an ordinary needle and embroidery thread, piercing the hyacinth florets (or pips as they are known in the trade) just as you would if they were beads. It's a fun idea for bridesmaids or even as an activity for little girls on a rainy spring morning. Next to that, the mirrored jewellery box holds double pink tulips that have been cut short. A small plastic carton inside has a little water in to keep the flowers fresh. To finish off this glamorous theme a pink freesia has been attached to a perfume bottle. The wonderful fragrance of freesias is unmistakable and is a favourite of all generations. The flowers were once only available in short-stemmed, multicoloured bunches, but now we buy them on long stems and in single colours as well.

On my way to work each morning, I pass Regent's Park. As spring arrives I look forward to the first colour appearing on the shrubs and trees. After months of greyness and damp, you can practically smell that spring is in the air. The blossom makes me smile as the brown branches burst with visions of sugar-pink pompoms dancing on the breeze. And – an added bonus – when the blossom starts to fall, petals fill the gutters and kerbside, just as if there had been a giant wedding with box upon box of pink confetti scattered everywhere.

Opposite — Astrantia flower heads are
so delicate. Star-like petals surround
hundreds of tiny stamens in the centre
of the flower. As well as pink, astrantia
is available in green, white and dark
maroon. It grows easily in the garden,
and for that reason it's ideal for adding
to an arrangement to create a very
natural garden feel.

Left — I've seen white ceramic vases
in the shape of wellington boots, so I
thought the pink rubber variety could
work just as well. Simply place a jar of
water inside each boot and add stems
of cherry blossom.

Project Pink and silver urn

This large silver urn is brimming with glorious spring flowers. Hyacinths with the palest complexion, freesias tinged with blue at their edges, calamine-lotion pink ranunculus, amaryllis, lilac and tulips whose lilac hue just breaks the sea of pink. Notice there is no foliage in sight.

Step 1 — Fill the urn with wet florist's foam so that it sits 10cm/4in above the rim.
Step 2 — Begin by adding flowers to the back and top, establishing your height with a grouping of lilac.
Step 3 — The stems of hyacinths and ranunculus are too weak to push into the foam, so use a strong woody stem from the lilac to make a hole in the foam first. Then push in the weaker stem. Gently brush open the ranunculus petals with your hand.
Step 4 — Use the flowers in groups rather than dot them through the display. This is my philosophy, to replicate the way in which they grow naturally.

Pink and feminine like lipstick or ice cream, these gorgeous flowers are irresistible to us girls. Imagine what their names might be if they were a range of lip colours: looking at the flowers from left to right, I've come up with Phlox Pink (the small flowers in the top corner), Delphinium Pink, Sultry Stock, Sweet William, Sexy Saponaria, Pretty Peony, Peony Pink, Passionate Pink (dark pink peony), Camiknicker Pink (rose), Flesh Pink (lisianthus), Raspberry Ripple (dappled roses), and finally Antique Rose.

Opposite — This is a fun take on peonies. In the early stages they are hard and round, their petals tightly packed, not yet ready to unfold. I've decapitated the flowers leaving no stem, and piled up the heads like delicious scoops of ice cream – creamy vanilla and ripe strawberry. Add oversized spoons or sundae umbrellas to complete the look, giving you a fun and frivolous table decoration.

Below — These classic pink roses on the point of opening are Dutch-grown commercial cut flowers. A huge amount of work and energy, not to mention cost, is involved in the development of a new rose.

The summer months provide us with a delicious menu of pink flowers: spires of pink delphiniums, glorious clove-scented pinks and banks of frothy hydrangeas. Tumbling clouds of perfumed pinky-white jasmine, wonderful trails of custard-yellow and pink honeysuckle, not to mention a glorious array of pink roses – from the palest hint of colour to the sharpest, most vibrant Schiaparelli pink.

Opposite — I love this image of a giant teacup and pink-iced cupcake. The teacup is packed with stems of sweet williams so that the flowers seem to float in a layer like raspberry tea. The cupcake is made up of several large paper cake cases. Inside is a very thin layer of florist's foam that holds the large open peony heads in place – the perfect pink icing. The cherry on top is a dark burgundy peony bud.

Above left — Dahlias are really gaining in popularity and rightly so. They are available in amazing colours and sizes – from petite coat buttons to teaplates – all with perfect precision-cut petals. They look great used en masse in the same tones, but a mix of garish orange-yellow and clashing cerise and red can be exhilarating.

Above right — This pink rose has an antique air due to its faded colour and the hint of green in the petals.

Opposite — Just look at this incredible dahlia. The mathematical accuracy of the layered petals is simply baffling – how does nature do that? The dahlia also has a particular fragrance; not a sweet perfume but a herbal one. Dahlias are very adaptable flowers: marvellously chic in a tall ceramic vase, but also nostalgic in an earthenware jug or wrapped in newspaper – the way my grandfather used to bring them proudly, freshly picked straight from the allotment.

Above — Bright pink acrylic boxes on a matching tray. One holds heads of celosia: like crushed velvet, they add texture to any display. Stocks of the same intense pink have been placed in the adjacent vase, their perfume more than making up for their short lifespan.

Project Peony and rose garland

This garland of peony and rose heads would be fabulous for a bride who wants something a little different. Small flower girls would look cute holding either end. Of course, it could also be hung above a doorway or laid down a long narrow table.

Step 1 — Cut a piece of string to the required length and then tie on a ball of string or twine at one end.

Step 2 — Cut the flowers approximately 12cm/5in in length and begin to bind them on, binding just below their heads, then carry on binding in the stems a couple of centimetres/ an inch down.

Step 3 — Continue until you reach the end, then reverse the stems so that you cover the bare parts and can't see the beginning or end. Tie ribbon on each end to make a bow.

Imagine presenting your daughter
with this little doll's house,
complete with flower garden.
I've used thornless stems of
blackberries (can you believe that
they are bred like this!) to climb
over the roof along with open
roses from which I've removed the
central petals to reveal the stamens
for a natural look. Rose petals have
been used to make a path and
whole rose heads fill the windows.

As autumn sets in, pinks in the garden start to deepen as if in
preparation for the cooler months. Of course, in the floristry
world things remain the same. We can buy soft pink roses,
gerberas and lisianthus throughout the year, but in autumn
other ingredients appear in pink, including dahlias, pink rose-
tulips, and wonderful deep pink hydrangeas. Every season brings
its own treasures to excite and entice us into the flower shop.
I tend to like deeper colours at this time of year, particularly
shades like burgundy – you can get some wonderful burgundy
anemones. Somehow, soft pinks seem to belong to those dreamy
days of summer…

Opposite — Tall birch branches at the entrance to a party venue. We painted the trunk and branches pink and hung them with jars of pink flowers. This is a great way to stretch a small budget. Once the trees have been painted, plastic pot and all, they require very few flowers. The alstroemeria on the highest branch has multiheaded stems and, as you can see, one head will fill the jar. The other flowers are nerines in two shades of pink. These are more expensive and more difficult to find. However, there are lots of alternatives, including pink freesias, spray roses, peonies, hydrangeas, tulips and gerberas. And that's only pink.

Above — A mesmerizing close-up of a shocking-pink nerine.

For me, pinks in winter take on a silvery icy hue, losing their summer warmth. There are still lots of pink roses to choose from, while waxy anthuriums take on a whole new lease of life, giving us longlasting arrangements while all around them other flowers are wilting thanks to the central heating! Pink lilies are terribly useful at this time of year, too, but the stars of the season have to be pink amaryllis. Available in several shades, they are sheer magic. Buy them in tight bud and watch them open into huge trumpet-shaped blooms.

As you can see from this picture, flea markets can be a great source of containers. I've combined this unusual 1920s Art Deco stand – I'm not sure what it was originally made for, as an ashtray, perhaps? – with 'Coolwater' roses. These are lovely large-headed lilac blooms that work beautifully with silver accessories. I think it's important to consider the style of the container and choose a flower that sits with a period piece like this. Roses are the perfect choice and right for the period because they are glamorous and decadent. This arrangement would make an ideal centrepiece if you want to raise the flowers above eye level. A small block of florist's foam was carved to fit the tray, then soaked in water. The stems of the roses were cut short, to about 3–4cm (approximately 1in), and arranged in a perfect dome.

Opposite — Hyacinths look beautiful attached to the bulb. They actually don't need to be planted in soil as the bulb holds enough goodness to produce a flower, as long as there is sufficient water. I have used broken pottery to support the bulbs above the water, toning the colour to the flowers. You can use all kinds of material to do this – pebbles, coloured gravel – but I thought the pottery would give an unusual recycled look that I haven't seen before.

Above left — Do you remember those Fifties hats made from feathers that would clip on to the hair? Well, here's my version, made from fluffy pink carnations.

Above right — This is just one of many pink tulips available. Look at its wonderful fringed petals with stripes of candy-pink, which open to expose powdery saffron-yellow stamens.

Blue

Louis Armstrong sang 'I see skies of blue and clouds of white', setting a mood of euphoria and exhilaration, yet singing the blues summons up a whole different emotion. The hues of blue are as varied as the images the colour blue conjures. Hateful bluebottles in their metallic jackets, weaving in and out in the summer heat; frozen blue fingers, icy from the cold; the blue of a bruise, fading to yellow and purple. A blue garden border has to be seen to be believed: towering spires of delphinium in shades from sky-blue to navy; cornflowers, clematis, sweet peas, nigella, scabious and thistles. As the Eurythmics' song goes, 'Sweet dreams are made of this…'

Opposite — Pansies have an old-fashioned charm. I've wrapped this pot plant in rough-textured craft paper and tied it with parcel string to echo the pansy's vintage style. *Below left* — These incredible 'Black Baccara' roses have been dipped into blue ink to intensify their blue/black tones. I'm not normally inspired by flowers that have been manipulated in this way but these roses really impressed me.
Below right — How kitsch is this? Traditional wicker baskets painted bright yellow and pink, filled with 'eggs' of muscari and forget-me-nots, made using florist's foam.

The 'blue bells' of fragrant hyacinths, tiny forget-me-nots and muscari (grape hyacinths) are the blue delights of spring. Anemones are around in spring and so, too, are agapanthus. Irises are another true spring flower that I absolutely love – not the everyday type, but the bearded varieties. I like the deep purple variety called 'Ziv'. You can buy bearded iris in spring but the lifespan is very short, although I think that's OK – in fact, for me, it's part of their appeal. Buy one or two and put in a place where you will see them constantly: by your bedside, on your desk or even in the bathroom to enjoy while you brush your teeth!

The vintage chocolate box on this page is exquisite. The box is so beautiful in itself, but it becomes irresistible with the addition of the truffle cases, each holding a little water and an individual primrose head of the deepest darkest blue.

Left — How delightful is this? Forget-me-nots in a lovingly made bird's nest that has been sprayed silver. Nest and flowers are tiny and so perfectly formed, that it's almost a piece of jewellery. Don't be concerned – the nest had long been abandoned and deserved to be saved. Never disturb a nest in spring!

Opposite— Think laterally: a vase doesn't always have to be glass or pottery. Here I've placed a bunch of lilac in a brass umbrella stand. A plastic bottle concealed inside holds water for the flowers.

On this page shades of blue run through flowers and containers. From left, the first container holds a single stem of flowering mint. More and more florists are using herbs to add fragrance to an otherwise unperfumed bouquet. The small purple daisies are in fact asters. They have been cut from a main stem that had many side branches and are available in white, lilac and purple. Commercially grown blue irises open their throats to reveal a flash of yellow. A single blue hydrangea head sits in a turquoise watering can; behind it is a vase of blue veronica 'tails'. An individual eryngium thistle sits on a narrow-necked vase, with an artichoke flower lying on the counter top in front. A tall deep-blue delphinium reaches up beyond the top of the page. The low blue goblet holds another hydrangea head.

Opposite — A tower of shallow glass bowls piled on top of one another. Each bowl contains a scant amount of blue-coloured water on which float tiny foil boats, with hydrangea, delphinium and gentian flower heads in colours that match the boats. An oceanic theme is not a new idea, so it does need reinventing. And I think this tower of glass and boats does just that.

Below — I remember our neighbours' gardens when I was a child full of blue hydrangea the ultimate suburban plant of the Sixties. That's how I always thought of it until, years later, I noticed other varieties and colour combinations.

Summer is probably the best season for blues. Think of hydrangeas, cornflowers, delphiniums and alliums. Tall aconitum or monkshood has hooded flowers like a sinister sort of delphinium in moody tones, but beware – they are poisonous. In complete contrast are scabious, gentle soft-petalled flowers that are as blue as the sky – I love them. Then there's flat-headed blue trachelium, in every shade of blue to lilac to purple. I like to put together a vase of all blue flowers, to see the variation in tones.

Below left — Hydrangea 'Ayesha' has heads made up of amazing mini flowers that have curly edges like lilac flower heads. The petals in this picture give an overall impression of purple/blue, but take a close look and you'll see the bruise-like tones. That's the only way I can think of to describe them: red and pink veins on dark purple petals, with yellow stamens to complete the effect.

Below right — A close-up of the individual star-shaped flowers that make up the globe of an allium head. I'm fascinated by the tiny elements that make up a bloom – these are like individual miniature flowers.

Opposite — Look how a dark interior wall and containers change the whole effect. To emphasize this moody atmosphere, I've used – from left – lilac phlox in a low container; above them is a wonderful dark purple hydrangea; next is a single 'Bluewater' rose and a bowl of purple veronica tails. Towering above, tall and proud, are lilac delphinium spears. On the right is a low, bowl of 'Ayesha' hydrangea heads and, taking centre stage in the foreground, a single cherry-coloured dahlia is in full bloom.

Project Have a heart

Why restrict hearts to Valentine's Day? This symbol of love and affection can be used for so many other occasions: attached to the doors of a wedding venue, a gift for a newborn baby, an anniversary token. Another traditional time for hearts to feature is at the death of a loved one. The moment you mention flowers for such a sensitive occasion people tend to clam up, but I think it's really important that flowers are able to communicate feelings at this time, saying all the things you are perhaps unable to say.

Step 1 — From a sheet of designer florist's foam (foam that has a waterproof backing), cut the shape and size of heart you require, then soak it in water. Cut flower stems short enough for the heads to sit closely to the foam. However, the stem must be long enough to remain firmly in place – about 2cm/¾in long should do it.

Step 2 — Start by filling in your outline with smaller-headed flowers, so you define the shape.

Step 3 — Fill in with larger blooms until the foam is covered.

I love blue flowers in autumn. Delphiniums are still readily available as cut flowers, along with clouds of blue hydrangeas mixed with gentle blue scabious, cornflowers and agapanthus. Personally I adore seeing a vase filled with just one type of flower, especially for a modern interior. But if you prefer a more natural garden look, then mix flowers just as you see them in the garden. It has always been my philosophy when arranging flowers for the house to reinterpret how I see them growing. I tend to group several stems of one flower together rather than using them singly. It makes a bolder statement as well as looking more natural.

A bag of the most amazing blue flowers, from the deep, purple delphinium to the pale lilac hydrangea. These flowers haven't been assembled randomly, there is a reason for my choice. I've used three different shades of blue, but also different shapes. This is an important consideration when choosing flowers. The delphinium is a tall flower and will provide the height in an arrangement. The gentian is shorter, but has buds that travel up the stem, rather than a mass of buds in one place, making it ideal for the edges of a display and at the front in lower positions. The large-headed hydrangea is a full-headed flower, possibly the largest cut flower we can buy. Use it towards the centre of a display to fill and dominate the central space. The eye is always drawn to the centre and it needs to be full. It's all a question of balance. I hesitate to use that phrase, as it's associated with traditional flower arranging and sounds too scientific, but it is a rule that I find generally works.

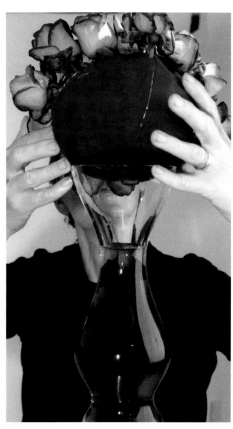

Project Blue pomander

To make this striking new interpretation of a pomander, I've chosen white roses that have been dipped in blue ink to create drama and attract attention. It's best to buy them pre-dyed where possible as it can be very messy to dye them yourself at home. The pomander could just as easily be made with alternative flowers such as carnations or peonies. I left a clear space at the top of the vase just to show that the water has been deliberately tinted as part of the design and that it's not seeping in from the flowers.

Step 1 — Carve two blocks of florist's foam into two hemispheres. Soak them in water before binding them together with florist's tape to form a single sphere.

Step 2 — Drop some ink into the vase to colour the water. Take care – you only need a drop or two.

Step 3 — To make life easier, begin to create the ball of flowers on your workbench. Cut the rose stems to about 4cm/1in below the flower head. Remove any foliage and cut the stems at a sharp angle. This will make it easier to push the stems into the foam and enlarge the area that takes up water.

Step 4 — Once you've made a start, push the ball of foam down on to the neck of the vase and fill in the remaining flowers.

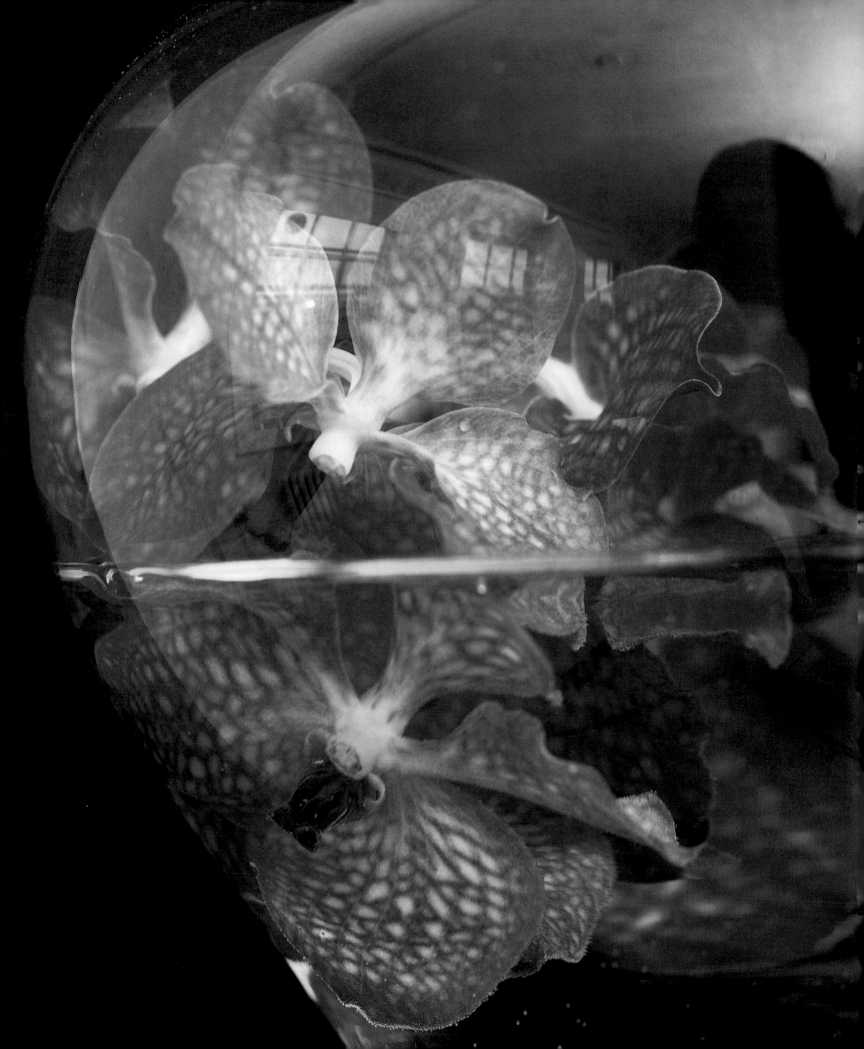

Opposite — Orchids are becoming increasingly popular and we're always in search of new varieties to keep up with the demand for something new. The wondrous Vanda orchid fits the bill – for the moment. Look at its amazing colour and markings (it's also available in a wonderful shade of apricot). This 'Blue Magic' variety shows how detail is magnified under water. The marvellous markings of the flower seem even clearer through the glass. *Below* — A glass urn holds an entire orchid stem. Half of it sits below the waterline: being submerged does not do the flower any damage.

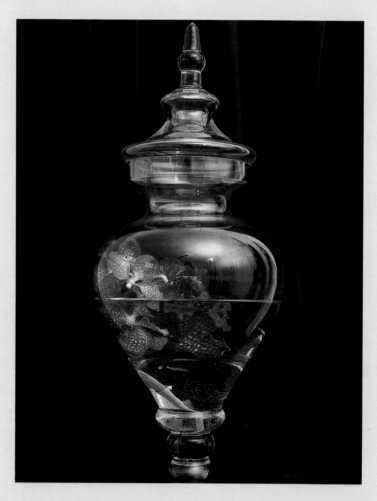

Blue can be a tricky colour to use on darker days or in a gloomy environment. For example, blue flowers in a church often disappear into the shadows, so look for the lighter paler shades of blue if you're planning a winter wedding. There's not an awful lot of blue to choose from at this time of year. But there are always blue anemones, which look great clustered into a fish bowl, their velvety faces peeping out with mascara'd eyelash centres. Purple orchids are pretty too, and will last for days, but be warned, they do come with a high price tag.

Above — Jet-black viburnum berries make an interesting addition to a display of flowers and they last for ages. This shrub produces delightful creamy-pink flowers in the earliest, coldest months of winter that work well in wedding bouquets.

Opposite — Freesia, a fantastic winter flower, is now available right the way through the year and its strong perfume makes it a firm favourite. It's available with a double bloom, too, and in a wide variety of colours: white, cream, pink, yellow, red and this pretty shade of blue. In this arrangement I love the juxtaposition of the glamorous with the mundane.

Flower directory

Page 14
Red **anemones** – see entry under page 19.

Page 16
These deep red **parrot tulips** are 'Topparrot'; other varieties to look out for include 'Rococo', 'Weber's Parrot' and 'Libretto Parrot'. If you buy tulips that have been dry-packed, you often find the stems floppy and unable to support the flowers. Don't panic. Simply recut the stems and put in water – they will quickly revive. However, they will stiffen in the position you leave them in. If you want them draped over the edge of the vase, that's fine. If you need straight stems, wrap them in newspaper before you stand them in water.

Page 18
Primulas are sold as pot plants and are typically winter and spring plants. They're widely available and come in pink, lilac, blue, white, yellow and orange, as well as red. The primula family is large; my favourites are the fascinating auriculas, with their 'antique' petals and dusty stems and foliage.

Page 19
Anemones (*Anemone coronaria*) come in many colours: white, soft pink, deep purple, burgundy and these red varieties, 'Marianne Red' and 'Mona Lisa Red'. Although spring flowers, they are on sale nearly all year round, apart from a short gap in summer. These red **ranunculus** in their scarlet ballgowns are actually members of the buttercup family and have layers of tissue-paper petals that surround a button of a centre. Buy them closed and enjoy watching them open over the next two weeks.

Pages 20–21
Commonly known as the **snake's head fritillary** (*Fritillaria meleagris*) because of its markings, this dainty little hood of a flower is supported by the most fragile of stems. Available only in spring, it's rarely seen as a cut flower, but more often as a garden plant. Larger species of fritillary in orange and yellow are also intriguing and have a strong herbal scent that's not everyone's cup of tea, but is definitely mine! *Begonia rex* is a houseplant that grows prolifically throughout the year. Its delicate paper-thin leaves have amazing silver, red and black markings with no two the same. Cut and teamed with flowers of similar colourings, they create a dazzling combination of colour, pattern and texture. These blood-red flowers edged with yellow are **gold-laced polyanthus**, a member of the primula family – see entry under page 18.

  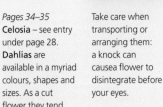 

Pages 30–31
Celosia – see entry under page 28. **Peonies** – see entry under pages 58–59. **Aster** – see entry under pages 160–161. Highly scented **stocks** (*Matthiola incana*) tend to be on sale in spring and summer in shades of red, white and purple. They are related to cabbages. **Eremurus** or foxtail lilies (*Eremurus stenophyllus*) come in orange, yellow and, more rarely, white. They are available for a short season in summer and can be up to 90cm/3ft tall. **Amaranthus** or love-lies-bleeding, is easy to grow in the garden and available commercially from June to October; the later in the season, the stronger and thicker the stems and tassels. **Sunflowers** (*Helianthus annuus*) are available all year round in different sizes and colours. **Fountain grass** (*Panicum*) has feathery heads on stems of 30–40cm/3–3½in.

Page 32
Celosia – see entry under page 28. The **guelder rose** (*Viburnum opulus*) has glorious red autumn berries, shiny and translucent. 'Grand Prix' **roses** – see entry under page 23.

Cotoneaster berries are a common garden shrub. They are renowned for their ability to survive in poor soils. All varieties are well-loved for their showy berries, and many Cotoneasters have attractive pink or white flowers too.

Pages 34–35
Celosia – see entry under page 28. **Dahlias** are available in a myriad colours, shapes and sizes. As a cut flower they tend to last for only about a week. Take care when transporting or arranging them: a knock can cause a flower to disintegrate before your eyes.

Page 37
Roses – see entry under page 22–23. **Celosia** – see entry under page 28. Redcurrants and miniature grapes aren't normally on sale in flower shops but don't overlook the beauty of using fruit in your displays.

Pages 22–23
Three varieties of **rose** are used here. 'Black Baccara' on the top tier, 'First Red' in the middle and the larger-headed 'Grand Prix' on the base. All these varieties have flat open flowers rather than pointed ones. You need this style of flower to make a success of the project.

Pages 24–25
Astrantia (*Astrantia major*) has clover-like flowers in deep reddish-pink and white. It is familiar as a garden flower, though a few varieties are available nearly all year round. **Celosia** – see under page 28. **Sweet williams** (*Dianthus barbatus*) have flat heads of tiny flowers in red, pinks and white. They come in mixed bunches when in season in the UK, which is April to June. You can get single-colour bunches from Dutch growers, but that makes them more expensive. A very long-lasting flower related to the carnation, they are summer flowers with a limited season. 'Circus' **roses** are striped floribunda roses with more than one flower per stem. Red **sweet peas** – see under page 26. Frothy stems of **astilbe** are available in shades of red, pink and white. **Dahlias** – see under page 34–35. A red variety of **hydrangea** – see under page 60.

Page 26
Commercially grown **sweet peas** (*Lathyrus odoratus*) have a completely different look from the garden varieties: the flower heads are bigger and the stems longer. These days, you can buy them in single-colour bunches. Sweet peas are still quintessential summer flowers with their unmistakable delicate perfume. Although these variegated **roses**, 'Soutine' and 'Intuition', are commercially grown, their markings give them the appearance of a garden rose. See also under page 136–137.

Page 28
Red bamboo is sold as cut stems around 50cm/19½in long. It's available all year round and lasts for months. Heavy-headed orchid stems such as cymbidium often need support, and by adding red bamboo you can make the support into a design feature, especially if the throat of the orchid is marked with red. **Celosia** (*Celosia argentea*) has woolly-headed flowers that grow on long stems. Its foliage does not last well, so it's better to strip away the leaves before using it. It comes in shades of red, purple and orange and has a lifespan of approximately two weeks.

Page 29
The **kalanchoe** plant has fleshy leaves and stems. The small star-shaped flowers are now available in various colours: pink, yellow, orange and red. You have to buy it as a pot plant and cut the flowers off yourself.

     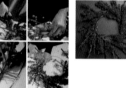

Pages 38–39
Ilex verticillata has strong dark woody stems that hold on to its glossy berries for weeks and weeks, even without water. It is available in golden yellow, too. Both forms are only on sale in winter. 'Grand Prix' and 'First Red' **roses** have been used here. There is an endless range of **gerberas** to choose from, not just in colour – from Barbie pink to chocolate brown – but in petal formation and size. The smaller versions are called **germini**. The eye or centre of the gerbera varies in size and colour, too – choose between brown and white. Gerberas are the staples of every flower shop, on sale all year round. **Anemones** – see entry under page 19. The **slipper orchid** (*Paphiopedilum*) has a fleshy flower that grows singly on the plant. Also available in green and white. A stem of cluster orchids, which also come in pinks, apricots and whites, is available all year round.

Page 40
Amaryllis (*Hippeastrum*) is a fantastic flower; large dramatic blooms with fleshy petals held aloft by thick tubular stems. They are available between October and May, in shades of red, pink, white, and peach. There are striped versions, too and the latest development from breeders is a miniature version. They last for more than two weeks as cut flowers, longer as flowering pot plants.

Page 41
Leucospermum (*Leucospermum nutans*), with their dense wiry tendrils on woody stems and brittle foliage, are native to Australia and South Africa. They last and last, drying in the vase, and are available pretty much all year round. **Anemones** – see entry under page 19.

Pages 42–43
Dogwood (*Cornus alba*) is also available in bright sharp green. Its leaves are large but papery; the real feature is its stem colour so it's best used stripped of its foliage. Cut to a specific size – here it's been tied around a plastic container – it will last for weeks, but will gradually shrink as it dries 'Grand Prix' **roses** are a longlasting, flat-headed variety.

Pages 44–45
Ilex verticillata – see entry under page 38.

Page 46
Arum lilies
(*Zantedeschia aethiopica*) have a thick fleshy stem. The flower is a cone formed from a single waxy petal. These are a miniature version very popular for weddings. Arum lilies are available in lots of lovely colours: pink, apricot, yellow, burgundy and orange, and are on sale all year round.

Pages 48–49
Straight stems of cultivated **cherry blossom** (*Prunus*) last extremely well. It normally arrives from the grower in 1m/3.9ft lengths, but can be found longer for larger displays. It is also available in pink; both appear in the market from November to April.

Page 50
Lily of the valley
(*Convallaria majalis*) has delicate bell-shaped flowers strung on a fragile stem of pale green. In the garden it flowers in May, but it's now available (at a huge cost) all year round, mainly because it is very much in demand for weddings. The forced variety still retains the same marvellous fragrance.

Page 51
Narcissus is a big family, with flowers of varying shades of white, cream, yellow and orange. These are paperwhite narcissi, available on long 30cm/12in stems that are foliage-free. It is truly a spring bulb flower but growers have now extended the season so that the first flowers appear in November and they disappear from our shelves around March.

Pages 52–53
Snowdrops
(*Galanthus*) are available in December in tiny but oh so charming bunches. Their stems are so small and delicate that it's difficult to mix them with other flowers – but why would you want to? They look so pure and simple as they are.

White

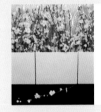

Pages 60–61
Hydrangeas
are available throughout the year in a wonderful range of colours: white, pink, blue, burgundy and green. Dip the heads into water and trim the stems before arranging. If they do wilt, try submerging them – stems, heads and all – in a sink or bath of cool water overnight or for at least two to three hours.

Pages 62–63
Peonies – see entry under page 58–59. White **veronica** has tail-like flowers, with tiny white florets that taper to a green point. It is also available in pink, blue, purple and cerise, and is available all year. **Larkspur** (a type of annual delphinium) has small flowers along the length of the stem. It comes in shades of blue, purple, red pink or white and flowers from June to August.

White **phlox** has clusters of yellow-centred flowers; they also come in purple, lilac and pink. Their season has been extended well beyond their natural summer flowering. The model, Lucy, holds an **allium** flowerhead, from the onion family. These spectacular globe-like flowers are available in summer in shades of pink and purple. **Delphinium** – see entry under page 152.

Pages 64–65
You will need to cut miniature **cyclamen** flowers and foliage cut from a pot plant; they're available in pink, white, red and purple, from October to around March.

Air plants are sold just as you see them; they don't need potting in soil as they survive on moisture and nutrients from the air. **Gourds** are sold in flower shops and markets only in autumn.

Page 54
Commercially grown **pussy willow** (*Salix caprea*) is available from October to April, an extension to its natural season. It comes on straight stems up to 1.8m/5.9ft tall.

Page 55
These white **tulips** with fringed petals are a variety known as 'Honeymoon'. See also entry under page 16.

Pages 56–57
Paperwhite **narcissi** – see entry under page 51.

Pages 58–59
White **peonies** (*Paeonia*) were traditionally available from April to June, but the season has now been extended to include October, November and December thanks to imports from New Zealand. My guess is that it won't be long before they're an all-year product. Also available in pink, peach, deep red and burgundy. **Eremurus** are more readily available in orange or yellow, which means you tend to pay a premium for white. See also entry under page 31.

Pages 66–67
These miniature **pears** (*Pyrus communis*) are golden-green but unripe – perfect for wiring and using in displays. You can buy these from selected florists only in autumn. Miniature **acorns** will come with foliage attached from selected florist's only in autumn.

Page 68–69
Chincherinchee (*Ornithogalum thyrsoides*) is very long lasting and available all year round. White **blossom** (*Prunus*) – see entry under page 48–49; paperwhite **narcissus** – see entry under page 51. **Phalaenopsis** orchids have fleshy butterfly-shaped flowers available in white, pink, purple and green. As a cut flower they last about three weeks; a plant will flower for approximately two months. They are available all year round. When buying **chrysanthemums** check the foliage along the stem – it should look fresh and green, not insipid, soft and wilting. They are available in a range of colours all year round. **Ranunculus** – see entry under page 19; **arum** lily – see entry under page 46–47

Pages 70–71
White **gourds** – see entry under page 64–65. White **hydrangeas** – see entry under page 60–61. **Eucharis** is a fleshy daffodil-shaped flower on a tubular stem. The buds open day by day: removing the old faded flowers encourages new buds to open. It's perfect for wedding work as the flowers are pure white and they're on sale all year round.

This shape of **chrysanthemum** bloom – with long thin petals at the edge – is called a spider and is extremely long lasting. The other variety in the display is 'Resolute'. The huge-headed white roses are grown in Columbia and are available all year round.

Page 71
Ranunculus – see entry under page 19.

Page 72
An open white **rose** with the centre petals removed.

Page 73
The flowers of the **Christmas rose** (*Helleborus niger*) are extremely long lasting, surviving for at least two weeks. The flower is also available as a plant. Both cut flowers and flowering plants are on sale only in winter. They are extremely expensive for a short-stemmed flower, but I suppose their rarity makes them a precious commodity when our gardens are at their most barren.

Page 74
Hydrangea – see
entry under page
60–61.

Pages 76–77
Green hellebore
(*Helleborus
argutifolius*) has
long-lasting flowers
on fleshy stems
about 30cm/12in
tall. It is on sale from
December to February
as a plant and cut
flower. The leaves
are large and slightly
prickly. **Fountain
grass** (*Panicum*) –
see entry under
page 30–31.
Alchemilla mollis has
lime-green frothy
flowers in mid-
summer that last
approximately one
week. It is an easy
plant to grow.

The **guelder rose**
(*Viburnum opulus*)
has lime-green
flower heads that
open into full spheres.
They're held on
woody pliable stems
and are long lasting.
On sale only in spring.
Buy potted **daffodils**
and **hyacinths** in
bud and they will
continue to grow
and open. Blades of
faded-green fleshy
succulent **agave**
hold their moisture
and last for ages.
Green **ornamental
cabbages** (*Brassica*)
are sold on short stems
or longer stems as a
cut flower.

Pages 78–79
The green version of
ranunculus is fairly
new on the scene
and not easily
available. It lasts in
the same way as the
more familiar
'tissue-paper'
petalled flowers
(see entry under
page 19), but
obviously looks
completely
different.
The miniature
widow iris

(*Hermodactylus
tuberosus*) is a real
rarity and these
delicate flowers last
literally for just a few
days, deteriorating
quickly. On sale for
a few short weeks
in spring.
This **auricula** is a
member of the
large primula family.
It's a member of the
gold-laced group –
just look at its petals
to see why. Primulas
are spring plants.

Page 80
Arum lily – see
entry under
page 46–47.
Yellow-gold
fountain grass is a
popular ornamental
plant that flowers in
July through till
autumn. The flower
colour changes
from whitish purple
to coppery purple
and persists well
into the winter.

Page 81
This garden
variety of
euphorbia is
quite hard to find
as a cut flower.
Beware – all
euphorbias have a
white sap that can
cause skin irritation.
Flowers around
April and May.
Hellebore – see
entry under
page 76.

Green

Pages 88–89
The **rose** 'Illusion' is
available all year
round. The flowers
arrive fully open yet
last for a further
two weeks in this
condition.

Buy **cabbage** leaves
from your
greengrocer in
season for this
arrangement.

Pages 90–91
Mini apples
(*Malus*) arrive in
October on thick
woody straight
stems that have a
mass of foliage and
apples clinging to
them. Once they
have fallen from the
branch, the apples
are still fresh
enough to be
displayed in a bowl.
Be inventive with
beautiful winter
cabbage: the
whole head can be

carved out to hold
florist's foam and
flowers or the
individual leaves
wrapped around a
container.
Steel grass
(*Xanthorrhoea
australis*) is straight
and strong – hence
it can be plaited –
and looks great in
tall column vases.
It is available all
year round.
Slipper orchids –
see entry under
page 38–39.

Page 82

A large **thistle head** surrounded by glossy hydrangea leaves, which are now available as a cut foliage.
A single **sunflower** (*Helianthus annuus*) with its deteriorating petals removed will last for approximately one more week.
Ornamental cabbage (*Brassica*) – see entry under page 76–77.

The side shoots from a tall **delphinium** stem are just too good to throw away – use them in smaller arrangements like this one. See also entry under page 152.
A single **poppy seed head** (*Papaver*), greyish green in colour, is what's left after the delicate petals have fallen. You can buy them dried all year round.

Pages 84–85

Poppy seed heads, including the 'Hen and Chicks' variety, are available dried all year round. These wild thistles have prickly stems as well as heads, so you wear gloves to handle them.

Page 86–87

Hydrangea – see entry under page 60–61.
Amaranthus – see entry under page 34.

Pages 92–93

Sunflowers – see entry under page 82.
Bamboo comes in from our foliage suppliers in 1.2m/3.9ft lengths and is cut to size. It is extremely tough – an electric saw is a good idea! It is available all year round.

Hydrangeas – see entry under page 60–61.
Snake grass (*Equisetum*) is enormously useful, not only in vases, but also as an outside binding and covering. It lasts well out of water.

Pages 94–95

Snake grass – see entry under page 92–93. White **roses** – see entry under page 88. Green **hydrangea** – see entry under page 60–61.
Sunflowers, minus their petals – see entry under page 92.

Green **chrysanthemum** blooms – see entry under page 68–69. Mini **apples** – see entry under page 90. Don't be afraid to mix flowers and fruit, like these sliced limes.

Pages 96–97

Skimmia is a glossy evergreen shrub that produces either green or red flowers in the autumn that last through to spring. As a foliage it's available all year round.
Catkins – the pretty tassels that hang from hazel (*Corylus*) branches in early spring – are a form of flower. As they develop they open and release bright yellow pollen. Catkins are available only in spring. This species of **magnolia**

(*Magnolia grandiflora*) is evergreen and has wonderful glossy leaves with brown undersides that are like suede. It produces the most magnificent blooms of waxy white flowers with a heavy perfume. The foliage is available all year round; the flowers are rarely on sale. The green variety helped to make **chrysanthemums** as a whole fashionable again. You can buy them all year round.

Pages 98–99

Lichen grows naturally on shrubs and trees. It tends to dry out after it's cut but can be softened by soaking in water.
Cyclamen leaf – see entry under page 64–65.

White **parrot tulips** begin their life with strong green stripes on their petals and continue to grow, opening to almost double the size. Look for strong green foliage when buying. See also entry under page 16.

Page 100
These yellow **tulips** are French varieties and have stems and heads that are double the size of their cousins. The tulips are available from December through to April in red, white, pink, salmon and yellow.

Pages 102–103
Yellow **arum lillies** – see entry under page 46–47. **Gold-laced polyanthus** – see entry under page 20. **Ranunculus** – see entry under page 19. French **tulip** – see entry under page 101. Three varieties of **narcissus** – see entry under page 51.

Pages 104–105
Gold-laced polyanthus – see entry under page 20. **Ranunculus** – see entry under page 19. Yellow **arum lilies** – see entry under page 46–47. Yellow **hyacinths** are a new variety on the scene (so, too, are the soft violet shades). You can buy them as planted bulbs or as cut flowers throughout late winter and spring.

A single flower from a yellow **cymbidium** orchid. The flowers grow up the length of the stem and are fleshy and long lasting. The orchid is also available in a miniature version and in pink, white, green, brown and cream. Two varieties of **narcissus** – see entry under page 51. Yellow **ranunculus** – see entry under page 19.

Pages 106–107
Cymbidium – see entry under page 105. **Narcissi** – see entry under page 51. These are our native spring **primroses** (*Primula vulgaris*), part of the primula family. **Ranunculus** – see entry under page 19.

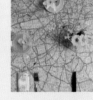

Page 114
Orange **dahlias** – see entry under page 34–35. **Marigolds** (*Calendula officinalis*) come in what look like huge bunches, but beware – the bulk of this will be foliage. The foliage has a wonderful herbal scent. Although individual flowers do not have a long life, the buds will continue to open in the vase. **Astrantia** – see entry under page 24–25. Mini **sunflower** – see entry under page 31.

Page 115
Golden-yellow **gerberas** – see entry under page 38–39. **Arum lilies** – see entry under page 46. **Centaurea** – see entry under page 110–111.

Pages 116–117
There are many **peony** varieties, but these huge-headed single ones are spectacular. At the moment they're available for a very short period in June, but I'm sure the availability will increase over the next few years, as they seem to be such a popular flower.

Pages 118–119
Orange **banksias** have wiry tendrils that create a ball-like flower, surrounded by crinkle-cut brittle foliage. The flowers will dry easily. They are available from late summer to winter. Orange '**Milva**' **roses** have petals that darken on the outer edges and last well as cut flowers. They are available nearly all year round. Orange '**Astro**' **chrysanthemums** have incurving petals of gorgeous gold; the flowers will last at least two to three weeks. They are available from late summer to autumn.

Yellow

Pages 108–109
French **tulips**
– see entry under
page 101.

Pages 110–111
Arum lilies – see
entry under page
46. The yellow
gerberas are a
variety called
'Cosmo'. See also
entry under page
38–39.
Yellow thistle-like
centaurea are
rather scruffy-
looking, with
equally untidy green
leaves. They're
available in May,
June and July.

Pages 112–113
Gigantic
sunflowers
– see entry under
page 31.

Pages 120–121
Gourds are purely
ornamental and are
not edible. You'll
find them in flower
shops and markets
in autumn.

The **pumpkins**, of
course, are edible;
look out for them
at greengrocers,
farmer's markets
and supermarkets
in autumn.

Pages 122–123
Parrot tulips – see
entry under page 16.
Poinsettias
(*Euphorbia
pulcherrima*) are
around from
October to
February, although
their value is in
decline immediately
after Christmas, as
they are seen as
plants to be given
during the festive
season. The
coloured leaves that
sit at the top of the

plant are produced
by controlling the
light levels. Red,
pinks and peach are
also available.
Daffodils are part
of the narcissus
family and the ones
shown here are
daffodils in the true
sense, the sort that
we all know and
love. Daffodils and
narcissi in general
do not do well in
florist's foam: in my
opinion they are
best used simply.

Pages 124–125
Craspedia has
yellow globes
suspended upon
the thinnest of
stems; it's available
throughout the year
and dries without
any effort at all.
Forsythia is prolific
in English gardens

in winter and spring.
Magically, growers
have stretched the
season and it's now
available from
August to May.
Strong, woody
stems support the
yellow buds that
open into star-
shaped flowers.

Page 126
The Sarah Bernhardt **peony** (*Paeonia lactiflora* 'Sarah Bernhardt') is a garden plant as well as a cut flower. It is only available in late spring or early summer. For best value for money, buy peonies in bud and watch them open.

Pages 128–129
Hyacinth pips removed from the main stem will last for a couple of days before wilting. Hyacinths are available as cut flowers or planted bulbs from late winter to spring. The stems of double **parrot tulips** will continue to grow, so you may have to trim them daily to maintain this arrangement. See also entry under page 16. **Freesias** are longlasting flowers, making them perfect for wedding work. They come in many colours: lilac, pink, white, cream, yellow, brown, purple and red. They have a strong perfume and are available all year round.

Pages 130–131
Astrantia – see entry under pages 24–25. The commercially grown pink version of **cherry blossom** (*Prunus*) with tall straight stems just like the white variety – see also entry under pages 48–49.

Pages 132–133
Tulips – see entry under page 100. **Freesias** – see entry under page 128–129. **Hyacinths** – see entry under page 128–129. **Ranunculus** – see entry under page 19. **Amaryllis** – see entry under page 40. **Lilac** (*Syringa vulgaris*) is available in a darker shade of purple, as well as white. Unfortunately, the commercially grown varieties have very little scent, whereas their garden counterparts have a wonderful fragrance. The straight-stemmed commercial varieties do, though, have a longer lifespan, lasting up to ten days. Growers have extended the season but you won't find lilac on sale in summer.

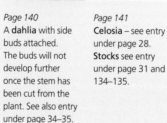

Page 140
A **dahlia** with side buds attached. The buds will not develop further once the stem has been cut from the plant. See also entry under page 34–35.

Page 141
Celosia – see entry under page 28. **Stocks** see entry under page 31 and 134–135.

Page 143
Peonies – see entry under pages 58–59 and 126. **Roses** – see entry under page 136–137. **Saponaria** – see entry under page 134–135.

Pages 134–135
Phlox (*Phlox paniculata*) has clusters of small starry flowers on stems of about 70cm/27in. Although a summer garden flower, it is available commercially as a cut flower throughout the year.
Delphiniums have tall spires of flowers clinging to a tubular stem, available for a short time in the summer months. They are also available in shades of blue and white. Wonderfully scented **stocks** have flowers that are round, flat and look as if they are slightly wilted. (You can tell if they really are: don't buy them if they have pale, wilted leaves.) See also entry under page 31.
Saponaria is a wild-looking, delicate-stemmed flower. It tends to wilt quickly out of water.
Peonies – see page 58 and 126.
Roses – see page 136–137. **Lisianthus** (*Eustoma*) is a long-lasting flower on sale nearly all year round.

Pages 136–137
At one time people hesitated before buying **roses**, as the heads so often wilted. Now we receive our roses in much better condition and as long as the stems are recut after purchase and placed in cool water, they will perform.
Peonies – see entry under page 126.

Page 138–139
Sweet williams – see entry under page 24–25.
Peonies – see entry under page 126.
Dahlia – see entry under page 34–35.
Roses – see entry under page 136–137.

Pages 144–145
Roses – see entry under page 136–137.
Hydrangeas – see entry under page 60.
Dahlias – see entry under page 34–35.
Stems of cultivated **blackberries**, grown without the thorns that rip your skin to pieces; they are available in July.

Pages 146–147
Nerines are available in various shades of pink and white. Buy them in tight bud and watch the petals open and curl back, to reveal the stamens. Pink shades are available throughout most of the year.
Alstroemeria is one of those flowers that fell from favour owing to overkill in the Seventies. But there are some great colours available and it lasts so well, that I think it deserves a comeback. The flower heads are gathered together in groups of four or five at the top of long stems. Remove flowers as they fade and the buds will continue to open.

Pages 148–149
'Aqua' **roses**, in their beautiful shade of lilac, are available throughout the year.

Pages 150–151
You can buy **hyacinth bulbs** with the leaves and stem beginning to show from around November to April. (Or buy them as a cut flower.) The flowers last for ages and have a truly fantastic scent that will fill a room.
Carnations suffered a similar fate to alstroemeria until growers reinvented them with new colours and revamped petals. They are available all year round in shades of pink, white, green and even terracotta.
Tulips – see entry under page 100.

Page 152
Huge **delphiniums** like this are available from May to November. There are thinner varieties available but to my mind they are rather mean-looking. Use them in tall vase displays or in florist's foam. They are a firm favourite for use in pedestal arrangements because of their height and stature.

Page 154
Pansies are available from September through to spring; there are some summer-flowering varieties, too, but they don't particularly enjoy the heat. They are such an old-fashioned flower but now available in all kinds of colours – soft pinks, apricots, yellow, reds and of course blue. Pick off dead heads and the plant will continue to produce buds.

Page 155
Black **'Baccara' roses** are available all summer. **Muscari** or grape hyacinths have dainty little fleshy stems to a maximum length of 15–18cm/6–7in. They have a delicate perfume and a short lifespan. Growers have extended the season but they are not available in summer. **Forget-me-nots** (*Myosotis*) have tiny blue flowers with a white centre. The stems are very fragile.

Pages 156–157
Primulas are available from October to May. They are hardy little plants that keep producing flower after flower and are available in a wide range of colours. See also entry under page 18.

Page 158
Forget-me-nots (*Myosotis*) have tiny blue flowers with a white centre. The stems are very fragile so it's best to use bunches and stems in water – they don't work well in foam. They will grow wild in the garden, seeding themselves year after year. As cut flowers they are available from April to July.

Page 159
Lilac – see entry under page 132–133.

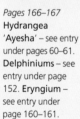

Pages 166–167
Hydrangea 'Ayesha' – see entry under pages 60–61. **Delphiniums** – see entry under page 152. **Eryngium** – see entry under page 160–161.

Page 168–169
Gentians have dark blue flowers arranged up a medium-length green stem. The flower shape is similar to that of a freesia, but without the fragrance.

Flowers appear from May and June. **Delphinium** – see entry under page 152. **Hydrangeas** – see entry under pages 60–61.

Pages 160–161
Mint (*Mentha*) is available from May to July and is easily grown in the garden – in fact, it can become a bit of a pest. **Asters** are available on long stems in a range of purples, pink and white all year round. **Irises** are available everywhere all through the year, in blue, white and yellow. **Hydrangeas** – see entry on page 60. **Veronica** has a long flowering season and its stems can be up to 60cm/24in long. **Eryngium** thistles have tall stems with a cluster of heads at the top and on side shoots. There are several different varieties available, some bluer that others, some with larger heads. They are available all year round. **Delphinium** – see entry under page 152. **Artichoke heads** (*Cynara scolymus*) are not around for too long, they tend to be here in late summer from July to August.

Pages 162–163
Individual **hydrangea** florets – see entry under page 60. Individual **delphinium** – see entry under page 152. **Gentians** – see entry under page 168–169.

Page 164
Hydrangea 'Ayesha' – see entry under page 60. **Allium** – see entry under pages 62–63.

Page 165
Phlox – see entry under pages 134–135. **Hydrangea** – see entry under page 60. **Veronica** – see entry under pages 160–161. **Delphinium** – see entry under page 152. **Roses** – see entry under pages 136–137. **Dahlia** – see entry under pages 34–35.

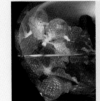

Page 171
White **roses** dipped in blue ink are perfect for a day or evening event, but leave them any longer and the ink will affect the lifespan and look of the flowers.

Pages 172–173
Vanda orchids are available as a cut stem or as a plant right through the year. The flowers are fleshy and about 4cm/1in wide, and are ideal for vase displays and for weddings. The flowers last for several weeks longer on the plant.

Page 174
Viburnum (*Viburnum tinus*) has matt green leaves, pinky-white flowers and these jet-black berries. The flowers are produced in winter and spring, the berries in autumn.

Page 175
The single variety of purple **freesia** is available throughout the year except July – this July gap is true of all freesias. Buy it in bud and enjoy the fragrance as the flowers open. The second and third buds should open, but not many beyond that. See also entry under page 128–129.

Index **Bold** pagination indicates Flower Directory entries

A

aconitum 163
acorns 67, **181**
agapanthus 155, 169
agaves 77, **182**
air plants 64–5, **180**
Alchemilla mollis 76, **182**
allium 62, 163, 164, **180**
alstroemeria 146, 147, **187**
Amaranthus 86–7, **178**
amaryllis 17, 40–1, 49, 132–3,
    148, **179**
anenomes
    blue 155, 173
    pink/burgundy 144
    red 14, 19, 39, 41, **178**
anthuriums 88, 148
apples, ornamental 90, 94–5, **182**
Art Deco stand 149
artichoke heads 161, **189**
arum lily
    green 80–1
    white 46, 69, **180**
    yellow 102, 105, 110, 115, **184**
aspidistra 88, 93
asters 31, 160, **189**
astilbe 25
astrantia 24, 114, 130, 131, **179**
auricula 79, 104
autumn
    blue 168–71
    green 88–93
    pink 144–7
    red 32–7
    white 64–7
    wreath 66–7
    yellow 118–21

B

bags 71, 110
bamboo
    green 92–3, **183**
    red 28, **179**
banksia 118, **184**
baskets 89, 116, 155
Begonia rex 20, **178**
bento boxes 94–5
berries
    autumn 32–3
    black 174, **189**
    red 32–3, 38–9, 44–5, **178**, **179**
    winter 44–5
bicycle 32–3
birdcage 125
bird's nest 158

blackberries 144–5, **187**
blue
    autumn 168–71
    spring 154–9
    summer 160–7
    winter 172–5
bottles 29, 76, 96, 129, 175
bouquets/posies 21, 34, 51, 90,
    97, 106
bowls 76–7, 108, 124, 150, 162
boxes 128, 141, 156–7
branches
    lichen covered 98, **183**
    painted 76, 77, 115, 146
    red 28, 34, 42–3
    white 48, 54
Brassica see cabbage
buttonholes 51, 99

C

cabbage
    ornamental 77, 82, **182**
    winter 88–9, 90, **182**
Calendula officinalis see marigolds
cans 19
carnations
    green 88
    pink 151, **187**
    white 59
catkins 96, **183**
celosia 24, 28, 30, 33, 34–5, 36,
    141, **179**
centaurea thistles 111, 115, **185**
cherry blossom 48–9, 130, 131,
    180, **186**
chincherinchee 68, **181**
Christmas
    flowers 9, 39, 72–3,
    122, **181**, **185**
    foliage 97
Christmas rose 68, 72–3, **181**
chrysanthemums
    green 88, 94–5, 97, **183**
    orange 119, **184**
    white 59, 64, 69, 70, **181**
cocktails, decorating 26–7
Convallaria majalis
    see lily-of-the-valley
copper beech 31
cornflowers 163, 169
Cornus alba see dogwood
Corylus see catkins
cotoneaster berries 32–3, 34
craspedia 122, 124, **185**
cups/mugs 50, 106, 138

cyclamen
    leaf 98
    white 64–5, **180**
cymbidium orchids 41, 105,
    106, **184**
Cynara scolymus see artichoke
    heads

D

daffodils
    green buds 76, **182**
    yellow 102, 103, 106,
    122–3, **185**
dahlias
    blue 165
    pink 139, 140–1, 144, 145, **186**
    red 25, 35, 165, **178**
    white 70
    yellow 114
delphinium
    blue 152, 161, 162, 163,
    165–9, **188**
    green 83
    individual florets 169, **189**
    pink 30, 31, 134, 136, **187**
    side shoots 83, **183**
    white 59, 62–3
dendrobium orchids 51
Dianthus barbatus see sweet
    william
dogwood 34, 42–3, **179**
doll's house 145
dyed flowers 170, **189**
dyed water 77, 86, 106, 151,
    162, 170–1

E

egg cups 107
Equisetum see snake grass
Eremus stenophyllus see foxtail lily
Eryngium thistle 151, 161,
    166–7, **189**
eucharis 70, **181**
euphorbia
    E. pulcherrima (poinsetta)
    122, **185**
    spring 81, **182**
Eustoma see lisianthus

F

flat containers 114, 162
foliage
    green 88, 96–7, 98

red 30, 31, 34
    white 66, 68
forget-me-nots 155, 158, **188**
forsythia 122, 125, **185**
fountain grass 76, 80–1, **178**
foxtail lily 31, 59, **178**, **181**
freesia 129, 132–3, 174–5,
    186, **189**
fritillary, snakeshead 20–1, **178**
fruit
    blackberries 144–5, **187**
    grapes 36
    lime slices 94–5, **183**
    melon/pineapple 30, 31
    ornamental apples 90,
    94–5, **182**
    pear wreath 66–7, **182**
    redcurrants 36–7, **178**
funerals 45, 167

G

Galanthus see snowdrops
garlands
    orchid and steel grass 90–1
    peony and rose 142–3
gentian 162, 169, **188**
gerberas 39, 41, 110, 115, 144,
    179, **185**
globe
    blue pomander 170–1
    green hydrangeas 86–7
    topiary tree 92–3
    white peonies 58
    yellow craspedia 122, 124, **185**
golden rod (solidago) 30, 31, 121
gourds 64–5, 70, 121, **180**, **185**
grape hyacinths 155, **188**
grapes 36
grass
    fountain 76, 80–1, **178**
    ornamental 86
    snake 92, 93, 94–5, **183**
    steel 90–1, **182**
    variegated 83
gravel 77, 151
green
    autumn 88–93
    spring 76–81
    summer 82–7
    winter 94–9
guelder rose (*Viburnum opulus*)
    76, **178**, **182**

H

headdress
    pink 151
    red 36–7, 45
heart shape 166–7
Helianthus annus see sunflowers
helebores
    Christmas rose 68, 72–3, **181**
    green 76, 77, 81, **182**
    white 72–3, **181**
herbs 160
Hermodactylus tuberosus see iris,
    widow
Hippeastrum see amaryllis
honesty 64
honeysuckle 124, 136
hyacinths **187**
    blue 155
    green buds 77, **182**
    pink 128, 132–3, 150, **186**, **187**
    yellow 104, 105, **184**
hydrangeas **180**
    blue/purple 25, 160–1, 162,
    163, 164, 165, 166–9
    green 74, 86–7, 92, 93, 94–5
    individual florets 162, 169
    leaves 82–3, **183**
    pink 136, 144
    white 59, 60–1, 70, **180**

I

ice cream cornets 136–7
Ilex verticillata 38–9, 41,
    44–5, **179**
iris **189**
    blue/purple 155, 160
    widow 78–9, **182**

J

jasmine 124, 136

K

kalanchoe 29, **179**

L

larkspur 62–3, **180**
Lathyrus odoratus see sweet peas
leucospermum 41, **179**
lichen 98, **183**
lilac 132, 159, 168, **186**
lilies *see* arum lily
lily-of-the-valley 50–1, **180**

lime slices 94–5, **183**
lisianthus 135, 144, **187**
logs 60
love-lies-bleeding (*Amaranthus*)
 86–7, **178**
lysimachia 62–3

M

magnolia, leaves 96–7, **183**
Malus see apples
marigolds 114, **184**
Matthiola incana see stocks
melon 30, 31
mint (*Mentha*) 160, **189**
monkshood 163
moss, alternatives 81, 93
moth orchids 69, **181**
Muscari 155, **188**
Myosotis see forget-me-nots

N

narcissi
 têête-àà-têête 66, 102, 103,
 106
 white 49, 51, 56–7, 68, **180**
 yellow 102, 103, 105, 106, **185**
nerines 146, 147, **187**

O

orchids
 blue vanda 172–3, **189**
 phalaenopsis/moth 69, **181**
 red cymbidium 41
 slipper 39, 41, 90–1, **179**
 supporting **179**
 white dendrobium 51
 yellow cymbidium 105,
 106, **184**
Ornithogalum thyrsoides see
 chincherinchee

P

paint
 autumn wreath 66–7
 branches 76, 77, 115, 146
 containers 80, 96–7, 116,
 155, 158
Panicum see fountain grass
pansies 154–5, **188**
Papaver see poppy
paper containers 138, 156–7
Paphiopedilum see orchid, slipper

pears, autumn wreath 66–7, **181**
pebbles 77, 151
pedestal arrangements
 red 30–1, 34
 white 70–1
peonies
 pink 116, 126, 135, 136–7, 138,
 142–3, **186**
 red 30, 31
 and rose garland 142–3
 white 58–9, 62–3, **181**
 yellow 116–17, **184**
phalaenopsis orchids 69, **181**
phlox 62–3, 134, 165, **180**, **187**
photinia 34
pineapple 30, 31
pink
 autumn 144–7
 spring 128–33
 summer 134–43
 winter 148–51
pinks 136
poinsetta 122, **185**
polyanthus, gold-laced 20, 102,
 104, 105, **178**, **182**
pomander, blue 170–1
poppy, head 83, 84–5, **183**
pottery shards 150–1
pram 120–1
primrose 106, 107, **184**
primulas **182**, **184**, **188**
 auricula 79, 104, **178**
 blue 156–7
 red 18–19, **178**
 see also polyanthus
projects
 autumn wreath, white 66–7
 berry wreath, red 44–5
 blue pomander 170–1
 dressed in flowers 62–3
 green globe 86–7
 heart symbol 166–7
 no bake cake 22–3
 pedestal arrangement 30–1
 peony and rose garland 142–3
 pink and silver urn 132–3
 topiary tree 92–3
 tulip bowl 108–9
 wrapped-up narcissi 56–7
Prunus see cherry blossom
pumpkins 64–5, 70, 118–19,
 120–1, **185**
pussy willow 54, **181**

R

ranunculus
 green 78, 79, **182**
 orange/yellow 102, 104,
 105, 107
 pink 132–3
 red 19, **178**
 white 69, 71
red **178–9**
 autumn 32–7
 spring 16–23
 summer 24–31
 winter 38–45
redcurrants 36–7, **178**
roses **187**
 blue/black 23, 27, 155, 165,
 170–1, **179**, **188**, **189**
 dyed 170–1, **189**
 green 88–9, 94–5, **182**
 no bake cake project 22–3, **179**
 orange 118, **184**
 and peony garland 142–3
 pink 135, 136, 139, 142–5,
 148–9, **187**
 red 22–4, 26–7, 33, 36, 38,
 41–3, **178**, **179**
 white 70, 72, 170, **181**
rudbeckia 121

S

Salix caprea see pussy willow
saponaria 134, **187**
scabious 169
shoes, bridal slippers 51
skimmia 96–7, **183**
skirt, white summer flowers 62–3
slipper orchids 39, 41, 90–1, **179**
snake grass 92, 93, 94–5, **183**
snowdrops 52–3, **180**
solidago 30, 31, 121
spring
 blue 154–9
 green 76–81
 pink 128–33
 red 16–23
 white 48–57
 wreath 66
 yellow 102–9
steel grass 90–1, **182**
stocks
 pink 134, 141, **187**
 red 30–1, **178**
summer
 blue 160–7
 green 82–7

pink 134–43
red 24–31
white 58–63
wreath 66
yellow 110–17
sunflowers **178**
 topiary tree 92–3
 without petals 82, 92–5, **183**
 yellow 30, 31, 112–13, 114
swan containers 54
sweet peas 25, 26–7, **179**
sweet william 24, 134, 138, **179**
Syringa vulgaris see lilac

T

telephone 40
texture 21, 28, 85
thistle 82, 85, **183**
 centaurea 111, 115, **185**
 Eryngium 151, 161, **189**
topiary tree, sunflowers 92–3
tulips
 green 99, **183**
 parrot 16–17, 99, 122, **178**,
 183, **186**
 pink 128, 132–3, 144, 151, **186**
 red 16–17, **178**
 white 49, 54–5, **181**, **183**
 yellow 100, 102, 108–9,
 122, **184**

U

umbrella stand 159
urn
 glass 79, 172–3
 painted 80
 pedestal arrangement 30–1
 silver 132–3
 white peony globe 58–9

V

Valentine's Day 39, 167
vanda orchids 172–3, **189**
veronica 161, 165, **180**
viburnum
 V. opulus (guelder rose)
 76, **178**, **182**
 V. tinus (berries) 174, **189**

W

water, tinted 77, 86, 106, 151,
 162, 170–1
weddings
 bicycle arrangement 32–3
 bouquets/posies 21, 34,
 51, 97, **181**
 bridal slippers 51
 bridesmaid's necklace 128, **186**
 headdress 45
 heart shape 166–7
 no bake cake project 22–3
 orchids 51, 90–1, **189**
 peony and rose garland 142–3
 winter 173
 wreath 66
Wellington boots 131
white
 autumn 64–7
 spring 48–57
 summer 58–63
 winter 39, 68–73, 122
winter
 blue 172–5
 green 94–9
 pink 148–51
 red 38–45
 white 68–73
 yellow 122–5
wrapped flowers 52, 56–7,
 140, 154
wreath
 autumn 66–7
 winter 34, 44–5, 97

X

Xanthorrhoea australis see steel
 grass

Y

yellow
 autumn 118–21
 spring 102–9
 summer 110–17
 winter 122–5

Z

Zantedeschia aethiopica see arum
 lilies
zinnias 88

Author's Acknowledgements

I cannot finish with this book until I have thanked all these involved… without their help, I'd still be working on it!

Of course, a big thank you to the clever Georgia for capturing the flowers and most importantly the colour in her great photography. The darling Lyndsay Milne, ever inspiring and supporting. Claire Murphy for deciphering my handwritten scrawl, Adam Walkden for delivering the text and prompting me daily (I could say nagging!). The lovely Lucy for modelling, Jonathan for his wonderful design for the book and gentle Sybella for quietly reminding me that the text was needed now! And METZ for their help with the project.

For Rebs and Lola too gorgeous for me to express, Brenda and Maurice my parents too wonderful to say, and Gary my absolute knight in shining armour. x

Published in 2007 by Conran Octopus Limited
a part of the Octopus Publishing Group
2–4 Heron Quays, London E14 4JP
www.conran-octopus.co.uk

Text copyright © Jane Packer 2007
Book design and layout copyright © Conran Octopus Limited 2007
Special photography copyright © Georgia Glynn Smith 2007

Publishing Director Lorraine Dickey
Editor Sybella Marlow
Copy Editor Sharon Amos
Art Director Jonathan Christie
Photography Georgia Glynn Smith
Stylist Lyndsay Milne
Stylist's Assistant Laura Fulmine
Production Controller Jane Rogers

British Library Cataloguing-in-Publication Data. A catalogue record for this book is available from the British Library.

ISBN 978-1-84091-485-6

Printed in China

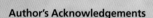